Sinatra

Night and Day
the man and the music

by
Fred Dellar and Mal Peachey

Designed by Will Harvey for JMP Ltd

First published in Great Britain in 1997 by Chameleon Books
an imprint of Andre Deutsch Ltd, 76 Dean Street, London W1V 5HA
www.vci.co.uk
Reprinted in 1998

Andre Deutsch Ltd is a VCI plc company

10 9 8 7 6 5 4 3 2

Printed in Italy by Officine Grafiche DeAgostini.

A catalogue record for this book is available from the British Library
ISBN 0233991794

THE EARLY YEARS

ALL OR NOTHING AT ALL
Spring 1939

THE BAND BUS gradually disappeared into the distance. Tears swelled. But there was no time for regrets now, decisions had been made and friendships put on hold.

Frank checked his watch. It was half-past midnight, Buffalo in the snow. No place to be for a singer intent on conquering America's airwaves. He picked up his suitcase, adjusted his coat collar and headed towards the hotel.

That night brought little real sleep. He relived the past, wondered what the future would hold. A future that involved a baby.

He thought back to 1935 and those days with The Hoboken Four.

They'd been The Three Flashes until Frank Sinatra came along. A vocal group ready to sing just about anything for a buck and a billing.

As The Hoboken Four they had gained a spot on Major Bowes Amateur Hour. Winning meant not only radio exposure but a contract with one of Bowes' touring shows. Not the greatest gig in the world. After all, there were sixteen other acts on the tour. But it was a start. Firstly though, they had to win.

No problem. The crowd that attended the broadcast from New York's Capitol Theatre on 8 September 1935, loved the quartet's version of Shine, even though they'd merely come up with a facsimile of the Mills Brothers' hit arrangement.

The stay with the Four didn't last long.

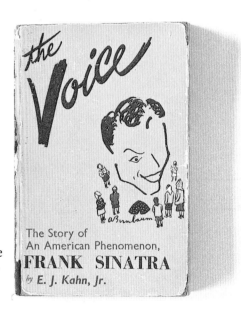

Before the year was through, Frank was back in home-town Hoboken, singing at local hops. By 1938, he'd settled into a spot at The Rustic Cabin, an Englewood, New Jersey night-spot, where he worked as singing MC and sometime waiter. Wages were meagre but the clientele could be influential and the job involved regular radio exposure. There was also the possibility that he might become the regular singer with Bob Chester's band, an outfit with which he sometimes rehearsed.

It was at The Rustic Cabin that Harry James heard him. James had been a trumpet player with the Benny Goodman Band. Benny was King Of Swing, a big-band mainman. And Harry, a flashy horn player well able to fashion a line of rabble-rousing pyrotechnics, had helped place Goodman in that position, proving one of the stars of Goodman's ground-breaking 1938 Carnegie Hall concert. In January, the following year, Harry moved off to form his own band.

It proved a crowd-pleaser and came up with an immediate hit with One O'clock Jump, a mindworm of a riff that Harry himself had fashioned in cahoots with Count Basie. But Harry was seeking something or someone that would provide the outfit with a commercial edge.

He found the answer one night when his band was playing at New York's Paramount Theatre. Lying in bed afterwards, listening to a radio shot by Harold Arden's Band from the Rustic Cabin, he'd caught a Sinatra vocal. Next night, James made the trip to Englewood, liked what he heard and duly signed the slim-line singer for $75 a week.

The Dream. The Voice, relaxing his audience.

FROM THE BOTTOM OF MY HEART
Fall 1939

JAMES WAS EASY to work with, everybody in the band loved the guy. As did Frank. Touring was a hard grind. But everything and everybody gelled, right down to their two-tone shoes. Frank was well featured on live shows and broadcasts. By July he'd even recorded two sides, From The Bottom Of My Heart and Melancholy Mood. Both the songs and the vocals were okay. No world beaters by any means. Around that time, Billboard's George T. Simon caught the band at a Roseland ballroom date and commended Frank for his 'very pleasing vocals' and 'easy phrasing'. Which was about right for the time.

There were other recording sessions, now for Columbia, throughout the year, pieced together in studios located in New York, Chicago and Hollywood, all the charts used on Frank's dates being shaped by arranger Andy Gibson. The eight songs recorded during this period included Gus Kahn and Walter Donaldson's age-old My Buddy, a vocal version of Ciribiribin, James' theme instrumental, and All Or Nothing At All. The last named, written by the team of Arthur Altman and Jack Lawrence, was a routine ballad and hardly memorable. But later, it was to prove of considerable importance in Frank's career.

Meanwhile, trombonist-bandleader Tommy Dorsey was having problems. For almost four years he'd employed Jack Leonard as band vocalist. A good-looker with a romantic image, he'd notched hit after hit with Dorsey, who led one of America's most successful big bands. But there'd been a falling-out between Tommy and Jack and in November 1939, Jack quit.

Dorsey hastily roped in a singer named Allan DeWitt, who just didn't seem to have what Leonard possessed.

The Dorsey band was working at Chicago's Palmer House at the time. Fortuitously, the James outfit with Frank was at the Sherman Hotel just a few blocks away.

Tommy had heard of Frank's growing reputation and offered a contract. Frank talked it over with James and then agreed to Dorsey's terms. Though Harry was loathe to part with his singer, he wanted what was best for Frank. And Frank was going to need the extra money that would come his way through working with Dorsey. For Nancy, his wife, had just gotten pregnant.

And so it was that the Harry James band coach deposited Frank in Buffalo on that snowy night.

Eventually he slept. And dreamt that he was bigger than Leonard, bigger even than Bing Crosby, then the most successful popular singer in America. Anyone can dream. Even a skinny wannabe from Hoboken.

The Sultan of Swoon showing why the babes screamed.

OH LOOK AT ME NOW
Early 1940

WHEN FRANK JOINED the band at a Rockford, Illinois gig, the guys in the band gave him the cold shoulder. Most of them were still mad at Jack Leonard leaving. They blamed the bossman, thinking Frank was Tommy's stooge. Frank shrugged. He'd show them.

Only Jo Stafford, lead singer with the Pied Pipers, Dorsey's new vocal group, seemed impressed.

'By the end of eight bars I was thinking, this is the greatest sound I've ever heard,' she told him later.

Frank didn't get much airtime on that first date, his solos comprising just two songs, My Prayer and Marie. The latter was a Dorsey hit that had originally featured Jack Leonard singing the melody straight while, to the rear, the band chanted in would-be hip fashion. The outfront fans liked what they heard and yelled for more. With no encore worked out, Frank and the band pieced together a version of South Of The Border on the spot.

By the end of the show, Tommy was smiling a lot.

Frank and Dinah Shore recording a charity release of Tea For Two.

POLKA DOTS AND MOONBEAMS
February-April 1940

RECORDS BY MAJOR popular artists were released with some frequency at that time – around two singles each month.

So Frank was rushed into RCA's Chicago Studio on 1 February 1940, to maintain the volume of Dorsey shellac needed to satisfy those who perpetually placed Tommy's records on the nation's best-selling lists. At the session Frank cut two sides, the unremarkable The Sky Fell Down, arranged by Axel Stordahl, along with Too Romantic, a cover of a Monaco and Burke song performed by Bing Crosby in Road To Singapore, the first of the ultra-successful Crosby-Hope Road movies.

Not that Frank had any connection with the Dorsey hits that graced the charts that month. The Starlit Hour and I've Got My Eyes On You featured the voices of Jack Leonard and Alan DeWitt respectively. The release of Bing's own version of Too Romantic ensured that nobody else was likely to sell their version of that song.

But Frank's fan base was growing, thanks to broadcasts with Dorsey that picked up hefty listening figures. While a New York recording session on 26 February provided little in the way of successful singles (though ironically Frank recorded I'll Be Seeing You, which he would revive many years later), he only had to wait until 4 March before a hit came his way. The song was Polka Dots And Moonbeams, which featured a gooey lyric but a gorgeous melody.

It was written by the new songwriting team of Johnny Burke and Jimmy Van Heusen, who would become house song-writers for Bing Crosby. Frank liked these

guys, they were young like him and hip. He needed men who could write songs for him. Frank understood already the need to have his own personality, his own sound and look. He couldn't do it without the right material. So old man Crosby could afford them now – he'd get his chance. Stordahl gave Polka Dots one of his classiest arrangements, and it zoomed up the charts, even beating out a rival version by Glenn Miller.

I'LL NEVER SMILE AGAIN
May-Fall 1940

FROM THEN ON, Frank's routine continued. Tours, radio shows, residencies, record dates and chart appearances, with Frank and the Pied Pipers gradually building in popularity, though Frank was annoyed they got little record- label credit, the releases generally being labelled With Vocal Refrain.

Even on I'll Never Smile Again, arguably the most popular record that Tommy Dorsey ever made, the vocalists were not credited.

The song had been written by Ruth Lowe, who'd played piano in Ina Ray Hutton's all-girl band but quit to marry publisher Harold Cohen. Cohen died suddenly, just a few weeks after the wedding, an event which inspired Lowe to write I'll Never Smile Again in his memory. The song, penned in 1939, was passed to Dorsey who opted not to record what seemed a maudlin offering and, instead, passed it on to Glenn Miller. Glenn, for once, failed to make an impact with the single. Finally, in April, Frank linked with the Pied Pipers and the Dorsey band to record Lowe's song. It was the first time that Dorsey had blended Frank and the vocal group on the same recording. But the bandleader didn't like what he heard. Another recording date was set for 23 May. This time Frank got his way, and more emphasis was placed on his voice at the session.

Frank felt good. He and Nancy had a daughter, Nancy Jr on 8 July 1940, while he was working with the band in Hollywood. Later that month, I'll Never Smile Again went to number one, and remained America's top record for three months. The only pisser for Frank was the fact that he had no label credit and even on the posters outside the theatres where the band played, his name and that of the Pied Pipers was listed below those of Dorsey's leading instrumentalists.

EVERYTHING HAPPENS TO ME
Fall 1940-September 1941

EVEN BEFORE FRANK had sung with the band, Dorsey had predicted that Sinatra would be as big as Crosby. So Tommy probably made the claim to enrage Jack Leonard – so what? By the fall of 1940, Dorsey could claim to be a leading clairvoyant.

If Tommy's band was reaping rewards as a result of Frank's residency as vocalist, then Frank too was finding his stay beneficial. 'You taught me everything I know about phrasing,' he told Dorsey, whose ability to play long flowing lines without seeming to breathe impressed Frank enormously. No other singer worked like that, it would be Frank's signature sound. For a while at least, the bandleader and his singer worked in an atmosphere of mutual admiration. Frank didn't get on so well with drummer Buddy Rich, though. Rich was forever getting at Frank. The bum once talked a young girl into asking Frank for his autograph, and when he signed she thanked him. Then, as per Buddy's instructions, added: 'Now, if I just have three more of these I can trade them for one of Bob Eberly's.' Eberly was Jimmy Dorsey's singer, and one of Frank's biggest rivals.

Frank heard the rumours that Bob, the brother of Glenn Miller's Ray Eberle (the two spelt their surname differently), was going solo, and he was worried. Eberly was probably the only guy who could steal Crosby's crown from Frank. He made plans to quit. 'It began to dawn on me,' he claimed, 'that if I didn't get out and become a soloist before Bob Eberly or Perry Como (then singer with Ted Weems's band), I would have to fight even harder to displace those guys and be number two.'

In September 1941, at a Washington DC date, Frank told Dorsey he was leaving, but giving a year's notice. Tommy just looked at him in amazement. 'He didn't believe me, he thought that I was kidding.'

When Dorsey came round, he got mad and said he'd do everything he could to block the departure. How could Frank ever forgive stuff like that?

Apart from the broken relationship with Tommy Dorsey, 1941 had gone well for Frank. In April, Dorsey's recording of Dolores, a song performed by Frank and the band in the film Las Vegas Nights, had topped the nation's best-selling lists, while during May, a college survey conducted by Billboard magazine named Frank as the most outstanding male band-singer in the States, ahead of Ray Eberle, Bob Eberly and Kay Kyser's Harry Babbitt.

That same month, a Down Beat poll found him displacing Bing Crosby as the nation's favourite singer, a position that Bing had held for the previous four years.

Then there were the records, like Everything Happens To Me, Violets For Your Furs (both penned by Dorsey staff arranger/composer Matt Dennis), and Ralph Freed and Burton Lane's freshly penned How About You, all of which would be reprised later in Frank's career. There was also involvement in a second Dorsey film, Ship Ahoy. They were filming when the Japanese bombed Pearl Harbor.

From that moment on the world began to change. Especially for Frank Sinatra.

STARDUST
January-August 1942

THOUGH STILL UNDER contract to Dorsey, Frank made four solo sides for RCA's Bluebird subsidiary in January 1942. Using arrangements by Axel Stordahl, he cut The Night We Called It A Day, The Lamplighter's Serenade, The Song Is You and Night And Day. Claimed Stordahl: 'Frank had a room in the Hollywood Plaza on Vine Street. We sat in it all afternoon of a sunny day playing the sides over and over on a portable machine. Frank just couldn't believe his ears. He was so excited.'

On release, Night And Day briefly moved into the US Top Twenty. Frank had his first solo hit.

While he worked on getting a solo deal with Columbia Records, Frank continued as singer with Dorsey, completing a career that would bring his tally of records with the band to nearly ninety in just two and a half years. During that time, Frank cut great songs like There Are Such Things, Daybreak and In The Blue Of Evening, but Dorsey also made him cut novelty crap like Snootie Little Cutie, I'll Take Tallulah and Dig Down Deep, the last being a plea for America's citizens to delve into their pockets and buy War Bonds.

On 2 July 1942 Frank recorded with the Dorsey band for the very last time. The venue was a New York studio, the arranger was Axel Stordahl, and the song – Light A Candle In The Chapel. Not that it was the final Sinatra-Dorsey release. Throughout the rest of 1942 and even during 1943-44, RCA continued releasing and re-releasing Frank's Dorsey material, There Are Such Things and In The Blue Of Evening becoming number ones long after Frank had left the band.

Frank couldn't do anything about it. He couldn't even record stuff for himself since on 1 August 1942, in protest against the number of jobs being lost to jukeboxes and radio record-play, the American Musicians' Union, headed by James Petrillo, imposed a ban on all recording sessions. The only exception were those for Armed Forces V-Discs that might help the war effort.

The ban could not have occurred at a worse time for a singer attempting to gain a record-buying public of his very own.

Polka dots were good luck, and Frank needed all he could get.

Frank showing Axel Stordahl how he wanted Laura to sound.

THE SULTAN OF SWOON

September 1942

ON 19 SEPTEMBER Frank finally became a solo proposition, but at a price. Tommy played hardball, making Frank agree that he'd pay the bandleader a third of all his future earnings as a solo act. On top of this, Leonard Venision, Dorsey's manager, claimed another 10 per cent. The only outlay that Frank felt good about was a weekly wage of $650 for Axel Stordahl, who agreed to leave Dorsey and become Frank's personal arranger.

Immediately, the press took its first long look at Frank when Benny Goodman began a four-week stay at the New York Paramount on 30 December. The joint ran film and stage shows, the film screened being Star Spangled Rhythm, a musical comedy starring Betty Hutton, Eddie Bracken, Bing Crosby, Dick Powell and Bob Hope. Frank was included on the Goodman show as an added attraction. But hordes of female Frank Sinatra fans brought the traffic outside the theatre to a standstill. Frank couldn't help but smile. During the show, hysteria reigned, girls fainted at the very sound of Frank's voice. Following the radio and press furore that followed, Frank was signed to play another four weeks at the

theatre which had become known as the Home of Swoon. Media interest intensified as cameramen and reporters moved in, detailing every aspect of the phenomenon – absenteeism from schools, the police who arrested queuing teenagers for violating a wartime curfew law, the candy-store owner who had to board up his shop because it was adjacent to the Paramount, and even ushers who complained the bobbysoxers left more urine on their seats than in the toilets. Anything and everything connected with Frank's residency at the venue made news. Frank's press agent, George Evans, had done one helluva job.

Fast turning into the biggest box-office draw in America, Frank became dubbed The Sultan Of Swoon, Swoonatra or, in an appellation that stuck, The Voice.

THE VOICE

1943

EVERYTHING WAS FALLING into line. The now 27-year-old Frank (his publicity hand-outs claimed that he was two years younger) was signed as a regular on CBS' Your Hit Parade radio series, singing the hits of the day. He followed this by gaining his own co-starring show, Broadway Bandbox, using the resident band of Raymond Scott, but with added strings and Stordahl conducting. During the year Columbia Pictures had released Reveille With Beverly, a slight but entertaining musical about a female DJ whose programmes appealed to local army bases. Frank's first film without the Tommy Dorsey band was great for networking. The DJ was played by Ann Miller, who would later co-star in On The Town; Duke Ellington and Count Basie made appearances, both bands with whom Frank would later record; while the Mills Brothers, one of the inspirations for The Hoboken Four, also appeared. The film's MD was Morris Stoloff, a name that would feature on future Sinatra-linked credits. Frank reprised Night And Day as his segment of the film, considerably enhancing the production's teen-appeal.

However, the problem of having no new records available due to the AFM ban proved a seemingly insurmountable hurdle.

Columbia, aware that Frank's records with Tommy Dorsey were selling in huge quantities, came up with an interim solution and decided that they too could cash in in similar fashion with their high-profile signing. Accordingly, they re-released All Or Nothing At All, one of the records that Frank had made with Harry James back in 1939. With no new material around, the fans simply went out and bought what was available.

All Or Nothing At All became a US number two.

Frank teaching New York kids the words to Star Spangled Banner at a UN fund raising event.

Though the record industry had stockpiled recordings in anticipation of the ban, no-one had imagined the situation would last more than a few weeks, the record companies supposing that Congress would declare the strike unconstitutional. But as time passed and the stocks dwindled, it became clear that something had to be done to keep catalogues moving. Frank couldn't wait to get ahead of the crowd.

If musicians couldn't play on his records, he'd record without them. His hand was further forced when Dick Haymes, the singer who'd succeeded Frank in both the James and Dorsey bands, made some a capella records using The Song Spinners vocal group. Haymes, an excellent singer, was a threat. When his single of It Can't Be Wrong became America's top record, Frank was forced to act. He too would make a capella records, using The Bobby Tucker Singers. Nine songs were recorded between June and November 1943, using the 'vocal orchestra' and arrangements sketched out by songwriter Alec Wilder and Stordahl, who, being an AFM member, kept pretty much in the background.

The first release from the sessions, You'll Never Know, reached number two while the B-side, Close To You, also clambered into the Top Ten. Who cared if Frank lacked orchestral backing? All that was required by the bobbysox brigade was the sound of The Voice.

And the chart success of such sides as Sunday, Monday Or Always, People Will Say We're In Love, Oh What A Beautiful Morning, I Couldn't Sleep A Wink Last Night and A Lovely Way To Spend An Evening (the last two stemming from Higher And Higher, a movie which featured Frank in a major role), proved that musicians, at least as far as organisations like The Slaves Of Sinatra and The Sighing Society For Sinatra Swooners were concerned, were totally irrelevant.

Two problems persisted. One was the flow of heavy payments to Tommy Dorsey. Frank had talked with the young Lew Wasserman, who had recently help set up a talent agency which was gaining in reputation. Lew, a friend to lots of Frank's other pals, had Jules Stein make Dorsey an offer he couldn't refuse. MCA bought Frank's contract for $60,000 and guaranteed the bandleader additional bookings.

The other was World War II.

THIS LOVE OF MINE

1944

AT A MEDICAL in October 1943, Frank was declared fit for military service. Not the kind of news likely to enthrall a singer just taking his first steps towards his own kind of world domination.

Then, at a later trip to a military induction centre during December, it was discovered that Frank suffered from a punctured ear-drum. The result? A downgrade from 1A to 4F and exemption from service duties.

Frank went back to work. A tour of the East Coast with Jan Savitt's band was followed by a trip to Hollywood for Step Lively, a movie which would provide Frank with his first starring role. By which time, there were two Frank Sinatras, Frank Jr was born on 10 January 1944, while his father was still making on-set love to Gloria De Haven. Ever active, Frank had no real need to take vitamins. Even so, when Lever Brothers' Vimms Vitamins division looked around for someone to host a radio show that promoted their product, they turned to Frank. The Vimms show, a half-hour programme, probably did more for Frank's burgeoning career than it did for the sponsoring

pick-me-ups and Frank took full advantage of the situation, using This Love Of Mine, a song he had co-penned with friend and manager-to-be Hank Sanicola plus song-plugger Sol Parker during his Dorsey era, as his opening, romantic theme.

Meanwhile, the AFM ban continued so Frank did his bit for the war effort. Unable to fight, he used his best weapon, The Voice, to cheer the troops. Besides some Hollywood soundtrack sessions, he completed several V-Disc dates.

V-Disc releases, described by one US serviceman as 'the next best thing to a letter from home', were 12-inch, 78rpm unbreakable vinyl recordings that were shipped every month to armed forces bases all over the world. Many of the records stemmed from special sessions or radio broadcasts and contained material that was never generally released. Frank who, in line with many others, received no payment for these records, considering his V-Disc sessions as part of his contribution to the war effort, was among the most prolific of the label's artists. From V-Disc's inception, through to the end of World War II, Frank provided scores of tracks for release, including such curiosities as There'll Be A Hot Time In The Town Of Berlin and Dick Haymes, Dick Todd And Como, the last named being a re-write of Sunday, Monday And Always that namechecked some of Frank's biggest rivals of the time.

Frank (far right leaning on piano)
stealing the scene from Tommy
Dorsey (left, white jacket) in Ship
Ahoy (1942).

SATURDAY NIGHT
(IS THE LONELIEST NIGHT OF THE WEEK)
November 1944

IT TOOK FRANK until 14 November 1944, three days after the two-year strike was concluded for Columbia, to line up Sinatra sessions that involved a real orchestra. A flurry of activity ensued in the pre-Christmas period, with Stordahl supplying brassy, swinging charts for Saturday Night (Is The Loneliest Night Of The Week) and I Begged Her and more filigree backings for the lovely I Fall In Love Too Easily and The Charm Of You, the last three songs stemming from Anchors Aweigh, Frank's film for MGM. Additionally there were two 12-inch sides – Ol' Man River and Stormy Weather, the first having proved a regular show-stopper for Frank in live shows, while Frank's onscreen performance of the latter would later form a memorable part of a future Jerome Kern biopic, Till The Clouds Roll By.

Frank felt free for the first time in his career. He could do as he wanted, without any interference from bandleaders or other vocalists.

This was the way to do it. From now on he was in charge. He sang hard enough to have fans seat-wetting at home, as well as at live dates.

Frank demonstrating his dark and brooding side.

THEMES AND VARIATIONS
1945

THE PUNCHY SATURDAY Night provided Frank 's biggest hit of his immediate post-Dorsey years, charting at number two in early 1945 but, by the end of the year, despite an array of hits that included Dream, What Makes The Sun Set, I Should Care, I Dream Of You, Homesick – That's All, along with two songs from the Broadway musical Carousel, You'll Never Walk Alone and If I Loved You, Frank had failed to hit the number one spot. Even Nancy (With The Laughing Face), a song written by Phil 'Bilko' Silvers and Jimmy Van Heusen in honour of daughter Nancy's fourth birthday, failed to move any further than number ten, despite being regarded by many Sinatra fans as a standard almost from the time that Frank introduced it on a Vimms radio show in early 1944. Frank recorded it at one point but shelved the take. Later, after receiving requests from servicemen who'd heard Frank's V-Disc version, he was forced to re-record Nancy, his new rendition becoming a hit in late 1945. The song, which then remained a staple part of Frank's shows for many years, utilised a marvellous Stordahl arrangement which most fans instantly recognised from its simple, beguiling string-set intro. Not that Frank relied purely on Stordahl's signature arrangements. He was already pushing and prodding in different areas, attempting to extend his range.

During 1945 he recorded two Latin sides with Xavier Cugat and four gospel-oriented tracks with black vocal group, The Charioteers. There'd even been one session masterminded by soon-to-be bete noir Mitch Miller, the songs involved being Just An Old Stone House and Old School Teacher, two compositions by Alec Wilder, a writer much admired by Frank. So much so that, as the year came to an end, Frank persuaded Columbia to record an orchestral album devoted to such Wilder themes as Air For Flute, Air For Oboe, Themes And Variations and Air For English Horn. The probability is that the project would not have gone ahead if Frank hadn't declared he would conduct the orchestra and suggested that the resulting album should be titled Frank Sinatra Conducts The Music Of Alec Wilder, thus ensuring maximum publicity and even reasonable sales for the release. 'I don't know the first thing about conducting,' Frank informed the outfront musicians, 'but I know this music and love it. If you work with me, I think we can get it down.'

Columbia's Manie Sacks, who had initially given the thumbs down to the whole unlikely affair, later confessed: 'Here were all these symphony guys with their goatees and their Stradivarius fiddles and one goddam thing after another. And Frank walks in and steps up on the platform like Koussevitsky, and by the time he's through, the musicians are applauding him and grabbing him and hugging him. I don't know how he did it but he made the most beautiful records you ever heard.'

Frank lending the NY Philharmonic support by guesting at a stadium concert. 15,000 bobbysoxers turned up to hear the longhairs. Frank ended the gig by thanking 'the boys in the band'.

OH WHAT IT SEEMED TO BE
1946

JANUARY 1946 FOUND Frank hosting the Songs By Sinatra radio show, sponsored by Old Gold cigarettes, the opening programme featuring guest star Peggy Lee. Such exposure hardly hurt the sale of Frank's singles, a number of show songs that included The Girl That I Marry, They Say It's Wonderful, September Song and Begin The Beguine all adding to his tally of hits. And, at last, he was able to boast a number one solo hit in Oh What It Seemed To Be, a song written by pianist-bandleader Frankie Carle in tandem with writers Benny Benjamin and George Weiss. The story of a love affair that began at a neighbourhood dance and ended with the perfect June wedding, the song, typically arranged by Stordahl, captured the hearts of America's romantics. Eight weeks after it first topped the charts, it was still there.

For the first time in his career, Frank felt the lyrics as he sang them. He and his wife, Nancy, were not seeing much of each other, and when they did, they'd often fight. Frank was being presented with all manner of female company as he travelled from coast to coast. He was one of the guys, he was young, maybe he'd married a little too young. His marriage was falling apart.

Even so, Frank's career continued on a high. As if to prove that Oh What It Seemed To Be was no fluke, he claimed another number one with Five Minutes More, a more uptempo affair with a lyric about a guy who'd dreamt about a Saturday date all week long and, having enjoyed his dream date, didn't want the night to end. Again, a Sinatra single proved a long-stay item, the record clinging to pole position in the charts for four weeks in a row.

In all probability, Frank was more proud of his recording of Rodgers and Hammerstein's Soliloquy. A difficult song that occupied both sides of a 12-inch single, it called not only for Frank to use the full range of his voice but also enabled him to demonstrate his interpretative powers. If ever a film was to be made of Carousel, the show from which the song came, then Frank was staking his

The Hollywood Bowl had it's first taste of screaming girls when Frank slayed them in August 1943.

claim for the leading role of Billy Bigelow.

Earlier in the year, another important record for Frank had briefly graced the best-selling listings. Titled The House I Live In, it stemmed from an award-winning short film Frank had made in 1945 to advance the cause of racial and religious tolerance. A flagwaver that now seems almost jingoistic in the manner it upheld American democracy as the way ahead to the outside world, it nevertheless oozed sincerity and struck a chord in that post-war world.

Not that Frank could have any complaints about his country of birth. For it was reported that he had just made his first million. But if he was a millionaire then he was an American one. John Wayne no doubt understood.

The year proved one of many highs – one supreme moment linking Frank with Nat Cole for the Metronome Poll Winners recorded version of Sweet Lorraine. But if there was ever an on-record low then The Dum Dot Song surely was it. Though the session that produced this monstrosity, formed the basis of a reunion with The Pied Pipers, the song – about a guy attempting to talk with a mouth full of chewing gum – still ranks among the worst ever thrust in Frank's direction. Even so, when released in mid-1947, The Dum Dot Song reached number twenty one in one US chart. Hits don't necessarily relate to song quality. Far from it.

Frank as the Kissing Bandit in 1948. He hated the film and made jokes about it for forty years after.

TIME AFTER TIME
1947

MAM'SELLE, FRANK'S ONLY number one of 1947, was a gentle, engaging love song that initially decorated the Tyrone Power-starring movie The Razor's Edge. Frank continued to raid Broadway songbooks in search of good songs with a guaranteed, and hopefully record-buying, public – registering with such as Almost Like Being In Love from Brigadoon, plus So Far and A Fellow Needs A Girl, both from Allegro. Deeper personal satisfaction, however, was achieved when Time After Time and I Believe, both from the Sinatra-starring movie It Happened In Brooklyn, provided a twin success, both sides of the single charting separately in the Top Ten. A Cahn and Styne song, Time After Time became an instant standard, one that would eventually be covered by a huge array of artists, ranging from Jack Jones and Dinah Washington through to Stan Kenton and Rick Nelson. The beauty of Frank's original version was that he didn't elect to grandstand – to go out on a gut-busting high note as so many chose to do. Instead, he concluded the song in quiet manner, providing it with the equivalent of a fond kiss. And though at times Frank would opt for a bravura approach, more often than not it was the manner in which he underplayed even the most emotional of songs that made them all the more relevant. Whispering 'I love you' in intimate surroundings has always been more potent than bellowing the same sentiment, in the mistaken belief that volume somehow equates with romantic impact.

If Frank's ability to select strong roles in films was questionable at this time – his lead portrayal in The Kissing Bandit was frequently mocked by Frank himself, while an attempt to emulate Bing Crosby's success as Father O'Malley in Going My Way, by playing Father Paul in Miracle Of The Bells, would have brought yawns even at the Vatican – in terms of records, his choices could hardly be faulted.

Perhaps the most memorable was a rendition of I've Got A Crush On You, a song with a somewhat twee lyric – 'I've got a crush on you, sweetie pie' – but one that, nevertheless, tugged at the heartstrings.

Frank's version, recorded at a brace of October dates that also saw the singer and Axel Stordahl piecing together versions of I'm Glad There Is You, Body And Soul, When You Awake and It Never Entered My Mind – was immaculate. Choosing to open with the verse, which provided added validity to the sentiments expressed, Frank's nigh-perfect interpretation of the song was further enhanced by the lyrical trumpet-playing of Bobby Hackett, a ploy that Tony Bennett doubtlessly filed away in his mind for future reference.

Hoboken declared 30 October to be Sinatra Day, just as Frank resumed activities on the Your Hit Parade show, co-hosting first with Doris Day and, later, with Beryl Davis. And even if one radio poll did name Frank second to Bing Crosby as The Most Popular Person On Earth (the Pope coming a poor third!), then Frank must have been more than gratified when his version of But Beautiful, a song from the Crosby movie Road To Rio and recorded by Bing himself, sparked the start of 1948 by reaching number fourteen, while Crosby's original stalled at twenty.

NATURE BOY
December 1947-1948

OLD PROBLEMS CAME back to haunt the record industry, when the AFM threatened another strike, scheduled to take place from 1 January 1948. With the result that the final days of 1947 found the various labels stockpiling once more and Sinatra and Stordahl recording some nineteen sides during December, including A Little Learnin' Is A Dangerous Thing, a double-sided, slyly amusing, aside-filled duet with uninhibited black nightclub performer Pearl Bailey, who'd starred in the Harold Arlen-Johnny Mercer Broadway musical St Louis Woman. It was a record clearly never meant for chart consumption but one that probably provided Sinatra, a Pearly Mae fan, with considerable personal satisfaction.

Frank thought that Nat 'King' Cole was the world's most fortunate singer. Sometime during the previous year, a barefoot bohemian named Eden Ahbez, who claimed to live on the hill below the 'Hollywood' sign, gave Nat a song called Nature Boy. A strange composition, it was somehow haunting and provided a kind of back-to-the-earth message to which listeners might relate.

Cole duly recorded the song with the Frank DeVol Orchestra, Capitol releasing it early in 1948. At which point it headed straight to the top of the charts and dominated the best-selling listings for the next eight weeks.

Faced with such a huge success, Capitol's rivals decided that they too wanted a piece of the action. Decca rushed Dick Haymes into a studio to cover the song, while Musicraft did the same with Sarah Vaughan and Columbia with Frank. But none could really compete with the Cole original.

Shirt open, head back, arms floating with the music, Frank in typical recording mode.

For the MU had called its strike and all rival renditions could only employ vocal groups to provide accompaniments. Frank's version, featuring the a cappella sound of the Jeff Alexander Choir, proved the most popular of the cover versions, reaching number seven in the charts. Its success was to some extent helped by the fact that Frank was able to perform the song, using a full orchestra, on the Hit Parade Show. Oddly, perhaps, many listeners, used to the recorded version, wrote in to claim that they preferred the choir arrangement. With the result that later Hit Parade broadcasts of the song all came a cappella.

With the AFM ban enforced virtually throughout the year, Sinatra spent little time in the recording studio. Even so, he could claim ten hits during 1948, all except Nature Boy having been recorded before the strike. Two of these tracks, What'll I Do? and the lightweight My Cousin Louella, stemmed from sessions with a trio featuring Tony Mottola, a guitarist who would form part of Frank's regular touring band even in the eighties. Experimentation was in. No longer would Stordahl's trademark strings be an obligatory part of a Sinatra session. Though the two remained constant companions, with Stordahl providing back-ups on radio and many recording dates, the partnership became more flexible, with Frank increasingly looking to outside help at record sessions. Changes had to be made.

ON THE TOWN
1949

IN JUNE, FRANK and Nancy had another daughter, Christina. In October the movie Take Me Out To The Ball Game wrapped up at MGM. But as far as Frank was concerned, 1948 had seen his career standing still. He even confided to his friend Manie Sacks, a main man at Columbia Records, that he felt all washed up. A poll published by Downbeat in January 1949 didn't help. It listed Frank in fifth position among male singers, the first time he'd dropped out of the top three since Dorsey days.

Though Stordahl, dropped from Frank's prime-time Light Up Time radio show, provided the arrangements on thirteen records during 1949, Frank also recorded a session with The Phil Moore Four, a combo similar in style to that of the Nat Cole Trio. Frank then recorded six sides with an orchestra conducted by Hugo Winterhalter, using arrangements by George Siravo on It All Depends On You and Bye Bye Baby and a chart by ex-Dorsey Sy Oliver on Don't Cry Joe. Additionally, Morris Stoloff, once musical mogul at Columbia Pictures, and Jeff Alexander were brought in as arrangers/conductors to change things musically. Stoloff masterminded a session which produced Just A Kiss Apart, Every Man Should Marry and the ultra-gooey Wedding Of Lili Marlene, Alexander took charge of a date that resulted in That Lucky Old Sun, a delicious re-working of Victor Young's Mad About You and Stromboli, a theme from an upcoming Ingrid Bergman film.

Even some of the Stordahl dates found Sinatra probing in order to come up with something different. Let's Take An Old-Fashioned Walk was a duet with Doris Day, with the Ken Lane Singers helping out, while The Hucklebuck, credited by some to George Siravo and with a booting sax solo from Herbie Haymer, was an R&B vocal revamp of Now's The Time, a Charlie Parker bop-era anthem.

The path was becoming more erratic and the hits less frequent, though 1949 reaped eight more Top Twenty arrivals for Frank, the tally including The Hucklebuck, Let's Take An Old-Fashioned Walk, Some Enchanted Evening and Bali Hai (both from South Pacific), Don't Cry Joe, That Lucky Old Sun and The Old Master Painter, a bright but slight cheer-bringer. Again, however, the list featured one must-avoid, the dire Sunflower, a puerile sing-along cut in hillbilly mode by a band that didn't (understandably) seek recognition. The song, backed by the superior Once In Love With Amy was issued in seven-inch microgroove form in December 1949, the first Sinatra single to appear in the new do-nut format. There were many who loved it. Not only the record-buyers that placed the ditty high in the charts but also the whole of Kansas, where Sunflower became the official state song. And maybe, somewhere, Broadway songwriter Jerry Herman began whistling the tune. For in 1964, he wrote the title song for Hello Dolly and everyone began asking: 'Where have I heard that before?'

It was during 1949 that Frank and Your Hit Parade finally parted company, Sinatra claiming that the split was due to the low standard of the material he was forced to sing on the programme. Not the most valid excuse from a man whose output had included such dire ditties as The Wedding Of Lili Marlene and Sunflower.

Filmwise, things were working out better. On The Town, an upper-class MGM musical that cast Frank, Gene Kelly and Jule Munshin as three sailors on a twenty-four-hour pass in New York, sported a fine score and garnered universally appreciative reviews for all concerned. Surprisingly, however, maybe because Sinatra was contracted to Columbia, no official soundtrack was ever released.

Frank studying the score while Axel fills in the musicians.

Nobody ever screamed
like this at Bing. New
York girls love Frankie.

Another event took place in 1949 that appeared to have no great significance at the time. Some months earlier in June 1948, Columbia Records had announced the arrival of the $33^1/3$ rpm microgroove process, making it possible for ten-inch records to not only contain far more music but also present this music in considerably enhanced sound. There had been albums before – usually comprising three or more 78 rpm discs housed in book form – but the LP, as it would become known, was an entirely different proposition: something that would allow artists like Frank Sinatra, whose musical ambitions ranged well beyond the restrictions of the three-minute single, to move into other areas and, eventually, attract a whole new range of record-buyers. Perhaps Columbia Records were aware of such possibilities. Early in 1949, they released the first commercially available pop ten-inch LP in the new process. Merely a microgroove reissue of The Voice, a four 78 rpm set originally released during 1945, it came in a flimsy pink paper envelope which was later replaced by a stiff card cover. But it had been recorded with microgroove in mind. It would be another year before Frank got around to recording his first 'real' long-player.

SING AND DANCE WITH SINATRA
Spring 1950

A DECADE AFTER signing to Tommy Dorsey, things were hardly panning out for Frank. The 1950s began badly. Mannie Sacks, the man who'd signed him to Columbia, decided to quit and move to RCA; George Evans, Frank's long-term press agent died and, on St Valentine's day of all days, following increasing reports of the singer's involvement with film star Ava Gardner, Sinatra's wife Nancy announced that she and Frank had separated.

Worse was to follow. Mitch Miller, who'd been a mainman at Mercury Records, became the new A&R boss at Columbia and set about revamping the label's image. He demanded and received total control, choosing artist, material, arranger and then personally producing the final product. 'When I went to Columbia, they were number four in the States,' he claimed. 'I took them to number one and many times we had eight records in the Top Ten.' A shrewd operator, his influence quickly permeated through the company. To Sinatra, however, Miller's arrival spelt trouble. He had little time for control freaks. Especially if Francis Albert Sinatra was among those they aimed to control.

During 1949, the year prior to Miller's arrival, Columbia had topped the US charts for just one week – with Les Brown's instrumental version of I've Got My Love To Keep Me Warm. But in 1951, following a period of reconstruction and various signings by the new boss, Columbia artists held on to the number one spot for thirty five weeks of the year.

Mitch realised that Sinatra was having problems. Frank's personal life was a mess, his association with MGM Pictures was coming to an end as he fought against what he termed 'life in a sailor suit'. And, during a show at the Copacabana on 27 April, Frank lost his voice completely and was ordered by his doctor not to sing for the next forty days.

It was around this time that Miller decided that Frank should record an album of uptempo material, which would emerge as Sing And Dance With Sinatra. He commissioned George Siravo to shape the arrangements and at two dates, on 14 and 24 April, just prior to Sinatra's vocal breakdown, eight sides were supposedly recorded live with a band, in keeping with the Union rules of the time. In truth, The Voice had no voice to speak of and the sessions were a total disaster from a vocal point of view.

But Miller, violating every rule in the AFM book, shut off Frank's mike, recording only the instrumental support on acetate. Later, when Frank was in better shape, the singer attended secret, after-midnight sessions when he added the vocals to Siravo's backing tracks.

The result was a wonderful, ground-breaking LP, Frank's first, and a precursor to Songs For Swinging Lovers, a release well ahead of its time.

KISSES AND TEARS
Summer 1950

FRANK HAD DECIDED years ago that no-one would ever control his career again, but here was this wiseass Mitch Miller demanding total control. OK, so the first six sides he'd recorded in 1950 – Chattanoogie Shoe Shine Boy, God's Country and American Beauty Rose – were three major hits. But the crunch had come when Miller had played Frank demo recordings of what he felt were two cert hits, My Heart Cries For You and The Roving Kind, and asked him to record them, using a fifteen-piece chorus along with orchestral arrangements made by Jimmy Carroll. Frank, who was anxious to catch a plane to Spain to meet with Ava Gardner, listened, and then angrily retorted, 'I won't sing any of that crap', before storming out. But the sessions, already booked, went ahead, with new Columbia signing Guy Mitchell brought in to take Frank's place, the resulting single proving a worldwide hit and one that sparked Mitchell's career.

Sometimes Frank's temper got the better of him. Other times he'd just go along with Miller to see what happened. He did agree to record with Miller's chorus on Goodnight Irene, a singalong version of a Huddie Ledbetter folk song. The song, like Nature Boy, was one of those phenomenal one-offs that occur from time to time. The Weavers had just recorded a version with arranger Gordon Jenkins, who Frank rated. And it was a monster, one that would eventually top the charts for thirteen weeks. Again the cover shots rolled in, and, once more, Frank did more than pick up the crumbs, his version reaching number five, the highest chart position any Sinatra record had achieved since Mam'selle in 1947. There were signs that the Sinatra record career might be reviving, despite the conflict with Mitch Miller.

Sinatra also recorded Kisses And Tears, a duet with bosomy singer/actress Jane Russell, Frank's co-star in the film Double Dynamite, and three others, Peachtree Street, Love Means Love and Cherry Pies Ought To Be You (all of which were real cute), with Rosemary Clooney. There'd also been some outstanding records with Stordahl, quality affairs such as April In Paris and Nevertheless which boasted a Siravo arrangement and a heart-stopping solo from rotund trumpet star Billy Butterfield. And if Sheila got banned in Australia, where the name had other connotations, so what? In Britain, where Frank headlined for two weeks at the London Palladium – his first-ever UK shows – he was mobbed by eight hundred teenagers, held at bay by sixteen policemen. It wasn't quite the Paramount all over again. Even so, Frank loved the adulation and the shows provided him with an opportunity to perform the kind of songs he wanted to sing. He was also hosting The Frank Sinatra Show on CBS television from 9 to 10 pm each Saturday night, a show destined to stay on air for the next two years. Things were not at all bad, Frank mused. For a time, at least, Mitch Miller could be forgotten.

A new decade, a new look. Girls stopped screaming, but women smiled. Frankie was about to become Danny Wilson.

WHY TRY TO CHANGE ME NOW?

January-June 1951

ANOTHER LINK WITH Britain was forged at the start of 1951 when one of Frank's singles London By Night/If Only She'd Look My Way was released in the UK as a fundraiser for the British Playing Fields Association, the disc receiving added kudos when the Association's president, the Duke of Edinburgh, donated a short introduction to the recording.

The first recording sessions of the year involved three songs from The King And I, the Rodgers and Hammerstein musical which was about to open at New York's St James' Theatre. The Sinatra-showtune equation had frequently resulted in a hit single in the past and this time, We Kiss In A Shadow, one of a trilogy with Hello, Young Lovers and I Whistle A Happy Tune, would make the grade, reaching twenty two in the US listings.

Also recorded at these sessions were Love Me, a somewhat nondescript Victor Young number, and I'm A Fool To Want You, one the few songs bearing the name Frank Sinatra on the songwriting credit.

The song had originally been penned by writers Jack Wolf and Joel Herron but Frank, deeply immersed in a soul-destroying love-hate relationship with Ava Gardner, altered the lyric to express his emotions. The result was one of the singer's most poignant records of the period. But in Mitch Miller's opinion it was one of the kind of Sinatra ballads 'you couldn't even give away'. Nevertheless, the record went Top Twenty despite competition from Billy Eckstine, the man known as The Sepia Sinatra, who covered the ballad without chart success, though it was rumoured that his version

outsold that of Sinatra's by three to one. It was the reverse side of I'm A Fool To Love You that proved to be the final bone of contention between Frank and Mitch Miller. A novelty song called Mama Will Bark, it featured Frank duetting with a superboob-bestowed dumb blonde known as Dagmar, who had appeared on Frank's show at the New York Paramount around that time. The record was just a fun thing, Frank yapping away in happy-hound fashion and fashioning what the lyric so rightfully maintained was 'the doggonist thing you ever heard'.

As with countless other Sinatra releases, both sides of the records charted, Mama Will Bark ending up seven places below I'm A Fool To Want You. Even so, Frank hated the record, which he later claimed 'was only fit for dogs'. Despite such problems and the manner in which he perpetually tore himself apart over Ava, aligned to the growing headache of investigations involving his possible Mafia connections, not everything in the Sinatra casebook was depressing. May 1951 was designated 'Frank Sinatra Record Month' by American DJs who invited their listeners to vote for their all-time favourite Sinatra songs, some of which would be used in Frank's upcoming movie, Meet Danny Wilson. Meanwhile, after months of staving off the inevitable, Nancy Sr finally announced that she and Frank were to be divorced.

Meet Danny Wilson, a man with the dangerous air of being on the edge.

The song is all. Farewell To Love was a personal message for Ava.

DEEP NIGHT
July-December 1951

FRANK HEADED INTO a Hollywood recording studio to cut a duet with Double Dynamite co-star Shelley Winters. The title? A Good Man Is Hard To Find. He was putting out signals to the still uncommitted Ava Gardner, around whose life he was shaping his own. Intent on marrying her as quickly as possible, Frank took an engagement at Reno's Riverside Hotel, his stay forming part of the six-week residency required for a Nevada divorce.

It was a time when friends were needed, friends like Harry James. As James was still signed to Columbia and fronting the powerhouse of a band, it occurred to Frank that linking with his old boss might result in a personally pleasing and eminently marketable single or two. In the event, James and Sinatra recorded three sides in July 1951 with Deep Night, a song by Rudy Vallee, proving the most romantically inclined of the three.

Farewell, Farewell To Love emerged as a searing, high-flying rendition of what, in other hands, might have ended-up as a late-night closer of a torch song, while Castle Rock, a R&B hit for Ellington saxman Johnny Hodges, could easily be included on any roots-of-rock sampler, the lyrics including a line about rocking around the clock. 'Go get 'em, Harry, for old times sake,' Frank yelled at one high-tension point in the proceedings. And Harry did just that, helping to create not only a Top Ten record but also one of Frank's most feisty releases.

Following this session, so full of bonhomie and good vibes, it was surprising that, within a few days, Frank should have been so depressed that he reportedly attempted to commit suicide.

It was Ava, always Ava. She had the power to make Frank feel like he ruled the world one minute, and was nothing but dirt the next. She made him feel alive, aching – while it hurt he knew it was real.

MEET DANNY WILSON
December 1951-March 1952

IN DECEMBER, MEET Danny Wilson was previewed in Hollywood, one review alleging of the film's plot: 'The resemblance to Sinatra's own career is more than passably noticeable.' Frank knew it. He wanted the film because of that. The plot of the gangster who helped Frank embark on a solo career on the understanding that he donated a high proportion of his earnings to the hood's bank balance, bore more than a passing resemblance to Frank's own problems with Tommy Dorsey. In March 1952, Frank played a series of shows at the New York Paramount, where the movie was being screened. But The New York World Telegram reported that the second balcony, capable of seating 750, remained empty and that, to most of the young girls at the stage door, the term 'Frankie', meant Frankie Laine, an artist whom Mitch Miller had taken with him from Mercury to Columbia, providing Laine with nine hits during 1951, including four Top Tens.

By this point Sinatra's own relationship with Miller had hit an all-time low. During 1951 he had recorded the majority of his sides – except for the notorious Mama Will Bark session – on the West Coast, to be as far away from the A&R man as possible. Eventually, things reached a point where Frank banned Miller from his sessions for Columbia. The bosses were not happy.

It was no surprise when the singer informed Billboard magazine that he would not be renewing his contract with Columbia when it expired at the end of 1952. But first, that contract had to be honoured. And, anyway, it was in Frank's interest to maintain a reasonable flow of chart records to impress any label thinking of offering him future employment.

WHY TRY TO CHANGE ME NOW?
March-September 1952

ONLY FOUR SINATRA singles sold in any appreciable quantities throughout the year. But then, Frank only took part in three major recording sessions during that period, these dates resulting in such sides as Walking In The Sunshine, Tennessee Newsboy and Bim Bam Baby, three songs that carried all the hallmarks of Mitch Miller involvements, being ultra-commercial propositions. But they also produced a stunning ballad in My Girl and a couple of brash but impressive blues-based offerings Azure-Te (Paris Blues) and The Birth Of The Blues, the last of which would become standard fare in Frank's onstage performances for some time to come. The final Columbia session, a split date with Mindy Carson who used the same musicians, occurred in September 1952. The only New York date that year, it linked Frank with orchestra leader Percy Faith and resulted in yet another superior ballad, Why Try To Change Me Now? Some perceived the title as a parting shot in Mitch Miller's direction, an on-record affirmation of Frank's claim that 'I ain't ever gonna change'.

However, those final sessions for Columbia, from the James dates onwards, were ample proof that Frank was changing. He was instilling even deeper meaning, a feeling of more involvement, in the best of the ballads, and his forcefulness and degree of swing on the more upbeat material stunned and surprised many of those who had been Sinatraphiles since the beginning. All that was needed now was someone or something to kick-start his career anew.

THE CAPITOL YEARS

LEAN BABY
2 April 1953

FRANK TOOK A LONG look around the recording studio. These guys had better be good. It was his first session for Capitol, his new record company, and the bums hadn't enough belief in him to cough up the dough to pay the musicians, the studio time, or even him.

It was just like it had been with Harry Cohn and From Here To Eternity. Studio head Cohn had wanted Ava for the movie, so he got her to come to his house for dinner. Ha! All Harry got was an earful about how 'that sonofabitch husband of mine' should play Maggio. So Capitol had only given him a year's contract. So what? Frank knew what he had to do, just like when he travelled 27,000 miles from Kenya at Ava's expense, to do the fifteen minute improvised (they didn't have a script for him!) screen test, for director Fred Zinnemann. They soon came back to him. He'd known that Maggio was made for him from the time he started reading the book on the set of Mogambo with Ava and Clark Gable. He played the drunk bar scene for Zinnemann. The sap had asked what a drunk does in a bar. Frank simply shrugged, pulled out a few Hoboken memories and made Maggio a sad barfly with a couple of dice in his pocket. That, and the fact that he'd do it for half what tightfist Cohn was willing to pay, while Eli Wallach wanted even more, meant that

Frank and Ava at the Academy Awards in 1953, at which he won his Oscar. While he was a loser, Ava was happy. When he got back on top, she wasn't.

Frank had the part. He'd already started on set with Monty Clift (who couldn't hold his liquor, but tried anyway), Ernie Borgnine and Burt Lancaster a month earlier.

Frank felt tired, but kind of happy. He knew what he had to do. It was a bummer that Billy May couldn't make it for the session. He liked his snazzy arrangements. Still, even though he couldn't persuade May to leave Florida for a day or two, Frank could try out one of his tunes. The arrangement by Heinie Beau was good. Frank looked across at good old Axel Stordahl, he knew he could trust him. He'd helped Frank through some of that crummy material Miller had forced on him back at Columbia and he'd been his best man at his wedding to Ava. Yeah, the tune looked good. But what about these words? Jeez, they looked a little goofy. Frank sighed. He nodded to Stordahl, 'let's do it'.

It felt good to be back in the studio, doing what he knew best. The sun was shining. Ava was being a real doll. And those mothers who didn't believe in him – Columbia records, CBS television, MGM studios and especially the ingrates at so-called 'talent agency' MCA (he'd earned them half a million dollars last year!) – were gonna be sorry they dumped him. Axel waved his left arm, two-three-four. Frank crooned. 'Doo, doo doo-doo, doo doo do', the brass swung in behind the strings. 'My lean baby tall and thin, five feet seven of bones and skin, but when she tells me, baby she loves me, I feel as mellow as a fellow can be.'

It was gonna be a while before Frank could really get into this. The key changes from major to minor were good, they fitted smoothly. Just these lyrics, man, did this Roy Alfred guy really think the kids wanted to hear this stuff? Frank shrugged. Billy May must've known what'd been done to his tune.

The orchestra ran through the song again, with Frank snapping and popping on the beat, scatting with the horns. OK, he thought, let's try it again. This time the singer dug deep, remembering times with Harry and the boys, his voice dropping to an almost raw shout on the second bridge, pushing against the beat, trying to make these cockamamie musicians swing.

Frank declared himself happy with the take. Axel smiled. Producer Voyle Gilmore knew better than to argue with his star. Sinatra might not be a Top-Ten scream idol any more, but his respect among musicians was legendary, and it wasn't a respect earned by the singer's fists. If Gilmore had a nickel for every horn player, pianist and fiddler who had a wide-eyed, admiring tale to tell about The Voice – as they still called him – he'd be a rich man who wouldn't have to work for a small, growing record company like Capitol – much as he enjoyed it.

In truth, Frank, Axel and Gilmore knew that Lean Baby wasn't going to relaunch a legendary singing career. But it was a good start.

The orchestra was puffing, yet Frank was breezing through Axel's arrangements. Gilmore called for a change of pace.

Bill Reid's I'm Walking Behind You had been chosen by Axel for its nostalgic feel. The way he saw it, the song had an almost tragic sadness, reminiscent of one of Frank's earlier hits, Someone To Watch Over Me. It was sung in the first person by a jilted lover following the object of his desire up the aisle as she weds another, pledging his undying love.

Gilmore, a former drummer who wasn't taken with Stordahl's dated approach, loaded reverb onto Frank's vocal to give him a ghostly presence. Frank agreed the effect was haunting, though to his ears a bit gimmicky. They had two songs in the can, neither of which was considered perfect by anyone present. Frank could feel things slipping away in an all too depressingly familiar way. He tried to pick up the pace again by turning to Rube Bloom and Johnny Mercer's Day In, Day Out.

The song was an old favourite of Frank's and would, despite this lacklustre performance, remain a source of inspiration and frustration in future recording sessions. Again Axel's orchestration was, to Gilmore's ears, a little limp. Maybe Frank felt it too, but he never let on to Stordahl. Instead, he turned to the second weepy of the day,

Frank the family man. With Nancy, Nancy Jr, Frank Jr and Tina in a carefully posed family publicity pic.

Don't Make A Beggar Out Of Me, an Al Sherman and Harry Goodman song. Frank thought it stank.

After listening to a playback of Lean Baby and Walking, Frank left the studio on a slight high. It had been a good day. Something was beginning to shape up in there, sure there were problems still, but by the time he came back at the end of the month, he'd have songs he really wanted, and maybe he'd get Gilmore to try for Billy May again. Axel had told him he'd been offered a job in New York working on TV with Eddie Fisher, that good looking kid who wanted to be the new Sinatra. Ha, who needed a new Sinatra? The original was still the best.

On his way back to Ava, Frank dropped an acetate disc of Lean Baby and I'm Walking Behind You with Nancy to give to their daughter. Frank knew that Nancy Jr would play it to her friends and tell him the truth about their reaction. Nancy Jr was thrilled. She liked her dad's version of I'm Walking Behind You almost as much as the version that had been played on the radio earlier that day. Eddie Fisher's version would be the big hit. Frank was magnanimous about it to his daughter. But he wouldn't forget. Ten years later Fisher would have cause to rue his untimely climb to the top of the charts with a song that Frank had chosen to record.

DON'T WORRY 'BOUT ME

30 April 1953

FRANK AND AVA had been through more in their four years together than most couples endure in a lifetime. He knew that. Frank recalled their meeting in February 1949, when he flirted with her in his new Lincoln convertible on their way to some picture shoot for MGM. She'd loved that almost as much as the yellow house in Nichols canyon where they'd first made love a month later. Frank didn't like Ava being indiscreet, but he'd kinda liked her saying that, 'Oh God it was magic. We became lovers eternally.' For a time it really was like heaven.

But why'd she have to be so like him? Foul-mouthed, angry and violent one minute, and then melancholic, reflective and self-pitying the next. If only they'd met at a different time, rather than when her career was sky-high, while his was sinking under a sea of bad press, novelty recordings and lame pictures.

Man! The fights, the sex, the drink, the making up. Sometimes it took so long to get round to the making up because she was so goddamned stubborn – so hot-headed. Like the time she had an abortion and didn't tell him. She was in Nairobi getting ready to make Mogambo, he was performing for the Democratic convention in Hollywood. Ava flew to London and terminated the pregnancy because, as she'd said, 'Unless you're prepared to devote practically all your time to your child in its early years, it's unfair to the baby.' She also knew that she'd be out of work if she went through with it, and didn't believe in Frank enough to know that they wouldn't lose everything if she wasn't earning money.

The next time he knew about it. It was only four months ago, Frank recalled as he prepared for a second recording session for Capitol. He couldn't do anything about it, though. He wanted the baby, thinking it might calm Ava down, allow him to be the master of their relationship. Maybe that's what scared Ava. So she went to London again, telling Frank, 'We don't have the ability to live together like any normal married couple.'

Well, he'd make her eat those words. They were trying again. While he was making Eternity in Hawaii, all he'd do was drink with Monty, pass out and have Mitchum and Debbie Reynolds put him to bed. Ava was working hard on a new film, Knights Of The Round Table. She was almost finished now, and told Frank she'd join him on his trip to Europe next month.

Frank was happy. He still hadn't gotten to work with Billy May, but Gilmore had brought in this Nelson Riddle guy. He was OK. Dino had said he was a bit quiet, but man, could he swing an orchestra.

Frank liked what Riddle had done with Nat King Cole and Dino, but was worried that he might slow things up. Gilmore had asked Riddle to score the songs in the style of Billy May – which he did so well that May ended up being credited for I Love You and South Of The Border. To let Frank see what Riddle could do himself, the session started with Harold Arlen and Ted Koehler's I've Got The World On A String.

The horns banged in with a sharp crescendo down a

Once he had the world's most glamorous woman on his arm ...

scale, holding low. Frank hit the cue perfectly, somehow sounding both cynical and hopeful. 'I've got the world on a string, sitting on a rainbow, got the string around my f-i-i-inger.' POW, the horns chimed. 'What a world, what a life, I'm in love'. At the age of 37, for possibly the first time in his adult singing career, Frank had hit on a song which reflected his inner feelings, and transmitted them with power and swing. He was in love, and man, what a life. His voice sounded wearily elated, the realisation that he was onto something grew throughout the song. By the time the orchestra was ready for the next number, Frank had it. Somehow he knew that the songs he wanted to perform spoke to him, about his life and troubles. Which meant that other people must feel it, too.

Don't Worry 'Bout Me, written by Ted Koehler and Rube Bloom, was a big ballad, underplayed by Riddle, allowing The Voice to reverberate across the strings. The horns glided beneath the words, which almost sounded like a private letter written to Ava. The middle eight, which was clearly scored to recall the emotive swing of Tommy Dorsey, had a harsh wall of horns building like a sob, finishing short of a cry as Frank repeated the last line with a tone of finality. 'Darling why stop to cling, to some fading thing, which used to be? If you can't forget, don't you worry 'bout me'.

When they finished the tune, Frank felt almost guilty. That was too real, better get back to the love affair. Riddle brought on his second Billy May impersonation (why'd he do it? The arranger never could recall), I Love You, written by Harry Archer and Harlan Thompson. Once again the horns swung into action, this time building a crescendo up a scale, before quietening for a walking bass accompaniment to Frank intoning 'I Love You is all that I can say'.

'I love you' – three words he's saying in the same old way, waiting to hear them back. The feeling was not quite as heartfelt, but the message at least was clear. Which was more than can be said for the last tune of the day. South Of The Border, by Jimmy Kennedy and Michael Carr, played like the soundtrack to a Western. Frank had sung the tune with Tommy, and liked it. This arrangement swung, at a moderate pace, with suitably Spanish horn inflections to go with the chorus 'South of the border, down Mexico way'. It was a narrative song about a Yankee cowboy hiding out in a small Mexican town who fell for a local girl, and took heed of Mission bells driving him away. Corny, but what the hey. Nice tune. Frank sauntered through it, finished and made plans to return in two days time.

MY ONE AND ONLY LOVE
2 May 1953

FRANK WAS HAPPY. Ava was definitely coming to Europe. It was perfect timing, she would get two months in England to finish Knights Of The Round Table while he would play dates across the country. Frank wanted Ava to know how she'd made him happy again. Anytime, Anywhere (Carpenter, Anderson) told her straight: 'It makes no difference what you do, I'll be true'. Nelson Riddle was shaping up as a good guy. His arrangement for Anytime was soft, understated, kinda like Axel would have done it, but with a thinner string section. Frank eased through the number, knowing that the big moment of the session was yet to come. Still, his voice sounded young again. He was gliding like Tommy's 'bone, holding on to notes clearly, no wavering. The omens were good.

Frank signalled to Voyle Gilmore that he wanted to go straight to the second number. My One And Only Love by Guy Wood and Robert Mellin, could have been a private, one-sided telephone conversation with Ava. Riddle let Frank do all the work, his arrangement adding colour and tone to Frank's cosying voice. To make sure Ava got the point of this one, Frank vowed never to record it again.

This was a defining moment. Frank knew he had it. This was a new, full sound. No-one else had done things this way, not even Dino. Frank felt at ease with these guys.

He was still paying them, but they didn't argue, they could take a joke and when he knew a second violin was out of tune, they corrected it. Frank had his confidence back.

Black suit, blue mood. Frank, the world's greatest saloon singer and the best-dressed man in LA.

The main reason for being so sure about singing was as a result of the praise he'd earned on the set of From Here To Eternity. Mitchum was a sonofabitch, but he was a great actor and seemed to like what Frank was doing. Monty was a strange little guy, couldn't hold his drink, agonised over stuff, but he too, was encouraging. And now Frank had finished the shoot, it was time for the easy bit – recording a song which, though not part of the film, would take its title and cash in on its success. Written by Freddie Karger and Robert Wells, the song had to have the same epic sweep as the film, which was passionate, tragic, lustful and deeply romantic. Nelson Riddle's treatment had to make the ballad work like the crashing waves of the credits. He went for a big, bold

brass intro that could have been any major studio's signature, and then settled into Frank's tender vocal. More than just another declaration of undying love, when the movie opened Frank knew, he would once again be re-evaluated by the public. He'd told Zinnemann that he was Maggio, that he knew the people in James Jones' book personally. Now the world could see and hear Frank Sinatra not as The Voice, but as a flesh and blood human being.

Frank finished the session with a passable version of Getzov and Frank's I Can Read Between The Lines, knowing that he'd produced three very good performances. Now it was down to Capitol to make them hits. He was off to Europe with his second wife for what she'd called a second honeymoon.

I GET A KICK OUT OF YOU

Summer 1953

HOW THE HELL did this happen? Frank was not happy. Ava was not happy. In London they missed the connection to Sweden. In Stockholm, Frank had a sore throat and drank tea with honey on stage to help him through the performance ('Crosby must have made this tea'). This evidently came over as a big insult to polite Swedes. In Naples there were a bunch of jokers at Frank's show who kept screaming for Ava, rather than listen to him sing. What could he do? He walked. Afterwards Ava flew to Milan. Alone. The press kept asking, asking, asking when they were gonna break up. What a bunch of mothers. And the fighting with Ava went on and on. They'd row, get drunk, fight and make up, it seemed, less and less. Christ, Frank would sure be glad when she'd be back at work.

London at least was a relief. Ava had Knights to keep her occupied, while Frank performed to very responsive crowds. The BBC were extremely courteous and respectful to Frank. He liked Great Britain. It was almost good for both of them. They stayed in a lot and made up. Until near the end of the tour, when Frank committed himself to a date in Atlantic City for early September and Ava refused to go with him. The gig was at Skinny D'Amato's 500 Club, which was in trouble. No big stars were agreeing to play the place. During Frank's absence, From Here To Eternity had previewed to ecstatic audiences. Skinny knew that an appearance by Frank would put the 500 back on the map for other name performers. Ava hated Frank's wiseguy pals and was suspicious of even Dino's friendship with Frank. She called Skinny and his pal Sam Giancana 'hoodlums'. Frank's loyalty to friends who hadn't deserted him when things were not going so good, was as fierce as Ava's dislike of them. Frank had to remind Ava Skinny had given him work when CBS dumped his television show a couple of years earlier.

Neighbours at the Sinatra's London apartment called the police when the discussion about who was what, why, and where, became too loud. Frank left the building, had a few drinks and returned to find himself locked out. Ava, meanwhile, had gone to a club with that creep Walter Chiari, who was sniffing around his wife too much. Frank was going to Atlantic City. Ava was going to Madrid.

(Opposite) Frank driving Nelson Riddle to peaks of perfection. (Above) with buddy Jimmy Van Heusen.

A FOGGY DAY
August–December 1953

IT ALWAYS FELT GOOD to be back among his people. Frank was at home with Skinny and his wiseguy pals. There were even made guys here. Back in New York in the early days, Frank had watched with awe, the respect handed out to the men with big rings and fancy clothes. Back then they dismissed the little runt with clothes too big and a mouth to match. Now here they were, in the 500, watching intently as he, Francis Albert, swung his way through That Old Black Magic, Birth Of The Blues and a couple of numbers he was planning to record in November, Cole Porter's I Get A Kick Out Of You and George and Ira Gershwin's They Can't Take That Away From Me. Frank held on to some old stuff for live work, things like Tenderly and Ol' Man River, but he was starting to create a new set out of songs he wanted to record, or just had. He mixed up the swingin' numbers with ballads.

In England he'd included the Gershwins' A Foggy Day which went down well for obvious reasons. And somehow it reflected Frank's mood. He'd record this too, next time in the studio. There'd always be one melancholic old favourite that he'd never give up, of course. Sat astride a tall, thin bar stool, wreathed in cigarette smoke and with his people dressed in their finery, Frank felt relaxed as pianist Bill Miller eased into the opening notes. This song was starting to take on a new life, maybe because it meant something to him.

Throughout the English tour this had brought the house down. Tonight, One For My Baby stopped everyone in their tracks. At the end of the song Frank must have thought he'd gone deaf. For a split second there was no applause. The crowd had almost been shamed into silence by the confessional interpretation of Arlen and Mercer's tune. As the sound of

clapping thundered onto the stage, Frank made a mental note. Must record that again, soon.

After the show, over scotch and cigarettes, Skinny introduced Frank to one of the most important Mafia bosses in America, Sam Giancana. Both men were impressed, and a mutual admiration society was swiftly formed. Sam, like other made guys Frank had met, knew Dino and loved the guy. No doubt, like all the rest, Sam asked Frank to teach Dino a bit more respect for where he came from. 'Don't he know we forgave him for stealing those dollars when he was a dealer for us?' Frank probably smiled and thought of Ava.

After Atlantic City, Frank made for New York, and picked up $6000 for appearing on Milton Berle's TV show, before beginning a month-long residency at the Riviera. Taking a suite at the Waldorf, Frank had lots of pals over after the show, when good and bad times were fully discussed. Mostly, it seemed, the bad. Frank was getting as melancholy as the Fall which swiftly enveloped the city. More ballads filled his set, more pictures of Ava were destroyed in the small hours, to be pieced back together again the next day. Without telling Frank, Ava flew into La Guardia expecting him to somehow know she was coming, and be there to meet her with flowers. Pissed off that he wasn't, she moved into the Hampshire House hotel across the Park. It took Frank's ma, Dolly, to make a reconciliation. She had them both over to her house for supper one night, and told them to stop acting like kids. Didn't they love each other? The next day Frank moved into Ava's suite at the Hampshire. It was short-lived. Frank was back with the boys in his town.

How could he return home to the wife after a show? She moved his things back to the Waldorf. Yet, they played the game for the press. Frank went along to the premier of Mogambo with Ava, and they both smiled. Straight after, she flew to Palm Springs. Two weeks later, on 19 October, Frank opened in Vegas at his favourite casino, The Sands. On stage, Frank could almost forget his problems. From Here To Eternity was earning praise from everyone, and he was being tipped for an Oscar. He was back to earning top dollar for live shows, and making all the right kind of new friends. He'd discussed with Nelson Riddle what they'd do at the next sessions, and they'd decided to make a complete long player, unlike any previously made. To Frank, the LP sounded like a great new challenge. Kind of like making a perfect live set, but in the studio. He'd just signed to make 26 fifteen-minute spots for NBC radio, titled To Be Perfectly Frank. At the Sands, all the new songs he tried out went down well.

Still, he was feeling kind of blue. Ava didn't make any of the Sands shows. Little wonder, Frank discovered the day after he'd finished his residency. On 27 October, Ava issued a press release through MGM, her film studio – the one which had dumped Frank – explaining that the couple were separating, and that she wanted a divorce.

The release read: 'Ava Gardner and Frank Sinatra stated today that having reluctantly exhausted every effort to reconcile their differences, they could find no mutual basis on which to continue their marriage. Both expressed deep regret and great respect for each other. Their separation is final and Miss Gardner will be seeking a divorce.' Ava said the release was 'the most honest and sincere explanation for our impending divorce'. Frank never publicly stated what he thought about it. He just wanted to die.

Frank, running on Vegas time, trying to adjust for TV. The glasses were essential ...

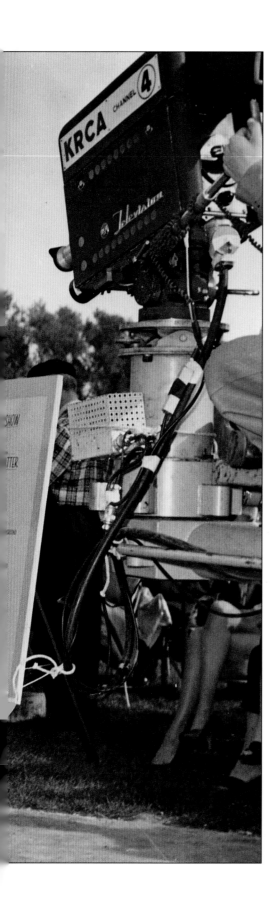

FOR YOUNG LOVERS
5, 6 November 1953

THE STUDIO WAS almost funereal. Frank, his hands pushed deep into his pockets, hat pushed back and tie loosened, leaned against the microphone. As if trying to get the last six months out of his system, he ordered the session to begin with A Foggy Day. Memories of happy times in London filled the light step through a melancholy tune. Frank sounded in perfect voice, his mood to match.

Holding at a steady pace, Nelson Riddle pushed his two saxes, four strings and rhythm section into Rodgers and Hart's skewed love song, My Funny Valentine. Someone had said it was about fags, all that stuff about Greek figures, they were all guys, right? Whatever, Frank was sad and longing for his funny valentine, weak mouth or no. How could anyone think he meant Ava with that line about looks being laughable, un-photographable?

The Gershwins' They Can't Take That Away was given a mean, dirtier treatment than Fred Astaire ever managed. Riddle's intro was all swirling Burlesque sax, Frank's first line a defiant statement. He might be no gentleman, but that didn't mean he couldn't remember with an edge to his fondness, and a sharp tone to his voice. It was supposed to sound like a warning, or a challenge should anyone try to take anything away from him.

At the end of the first day, Frank began to let the heartache bite. It was the third time he'd recorded Dennis and Adair's Violets For Your Furs, but this was the first time it really meant something to him. The song, a first-person narrative, described a cold Manhattan day on which the lovestruck singer bought violets for his love. Suddenly mid-winter became spring and the couple fell in love completely. Frank's final line almost sounded as if he was about to break down. Gilmore halted the session, Riddle took Frank home.

The next day Frank's mood hadn't shifted. He wanted to do Like Someone In Love. Ever the pro, he knew his mood would make the song better than even Johnny Burke and Jimmy Van Heusen had thought. Riddle's strings pluck along in an almost mocking, jaunty step, until the final chorus when even they succumb to Frank's heartache and swoon out the number.

Unable to take too much of the blues, Riddle suggested a false start on Cole Porter's I Get A Kick Out Of You. Frank liked the idea, and the first verse was performed in an almost unrecognisably downbeat manner, before the signature chorus kicked in – although not with any great spirit at first. Frank sounded as if he really had gotten a kick – in the head – from the object of his love.

Unable to sustain any pretence of jollity, Frank demanded that Rodgers and Hart's Little Girl Blue was next. He might have been forgiven for revelling in lines like 'just sit there and count the raindrops falling on you, it's time you knew, all you can count on, are the raindrops that fall on, Little Girl Blue'.

He didn't. Like with the rest of the session, Frank just sounded sad.

Determined, however, that the session would not end on such an emotional low point, Frank and Riddle went for Blane and Martin's The Girl Next Door as the final cut of the day. Frank couldn't help but think about Nancy. The childhood sweetheart who never argued, always supported him, gave life to his children and even now would not bad mouth him or tell him how dumb he's being. Nancy, like the girl of the song, was tender, sweet and ever hopeful. Frank looked around the room. Musicians were leaning back, shirtsleeves rolled up, instruments hanging loosely by their side. There it was. In two days Frank had created a complete album, his first for Capitol. It wasn't a brilliant beginning, but Hell, it was damned good. Frank liked it that Songs For Young Lovers was kinda like a film. It had a mood – a beginning, middle and end. For the sleeve, Frank was pictured standing alone under a streetlamp, cigarette in hand, watching couples pass by. As Maggio he'd been, what did Monty call him? Yeah. A fallible hero. In Songs For Young Lovers, just like in From Here To Eternity, Frank was playing himself, or at least one side of himself. These eight songs had such a sad air, being sung by a man alone. Man, he felt alone now that Ava had flown the coop. Frank knew that these songs showed him as he was – approaching middle age, knowing a thing or two about life but, like every other guy he knew, they showed how little he knew about women. Except that it was wonderful to have, and hurt a lot to have not.

YOUNG AT HEART
8, 9 December 1953

MAN! WHAT A RIDE. Frank was bushed. Dino, Sammy and the guys hadn't let him alone for the past two weeks. Those stupid bums in the press had printed lies about him trying to kill himself, again! Aaah, what bull. He'd just been working too hard, and wasn't so happy that Ava was in Spain with some dumb bullfighter. Well, we'd see how the guy handled a grown man with two fists. It was a shame he'd miss Christmas with the kids, but there'd be plenty of others. He can't have a broad treating him this way. Dino had laughed and told him he was mad. Maybe he was. He was here in the studio again, which was pretty skewed. But he had an idea to have a crack at that wiseass Martin.

First he needed to warm up. He'd liked David Raskin and Dok Stanford's optimistic ditty about a betting man's view on love, Take A Chance. It sounded like something Sammy might do, which was fine – he could have it after Frank. It was a pleasant enough song, jaunty, upbeat. Frank almost felt convinced by it.

The real business of the day was up next. He and Dino shared a mutual respect for Crosby, who inspired both men. Frank thought he 'inspired' Martin more, and had laughed about some of his pal's recent record releases, particularly If I Could Sing Like Bing. Frank thought it would be funny to do a number like Dino. MacIntyre and Ferre's Ya Better Stop was perfect. It was the right tempo and pitch for Frank to do a Dino. And the title was spot-on, too. Wasn't his dago pal always yelling, 'Ya gotta stop, you're killing me!'

Frank loved the line that ran, 'I'm no novice at this making love, in a sly way, try it my way, why don't you get this show on the highway'. Dino always had some broad, usually two, waiting at a motel somewhere while Jeannette cooked dinner for him. Frank could hardly keep from laughing. He even ended the number with

If I Could Sing Like ... Dino. Frank taking off Dag for a version of Ya Better Stop.

a mock-Martin shout of, 'Ah here now this ain't gonna be another one of those fade away records! Get your grimy hand off that dial, man.'

Frank was happy. For Miller and Conn's Why Should I Cry, Riddle had created an oddly upbeat arrangement for a song which had its narrator in a similar predicament to Frank. The horns had a jazzy, almost burlesque feel. Frank couldn't put any feeling into the words, not yet, anyway. He knew why he should cry over Ava. Asking the question in a challenging way didn't fit right, but the song swung. So did Frank, and it had been a good day. Tomorrow would be tougher.

The next morning, the weather was terrible and inside the studio Riddle had worked raindrops onto the front of Robert Mellin and George Finlay's Rain (Falling From The Sky). The strings swelled enough to make Axel proud. Frank pleaded with the rain to wash away his tears. He'd gotten some sleep after yesterday's session, so he was in stronger voice. It was a gentle beginning to the day's work.

From the opening string swell outlining the melody of Johnny Richards and Carolyn Leigh's Young At Heart, Frank knew the song was a hit. He wanted to make it a personal message to all those other big kids out there who had had enough of cold wars, communists, the A Bomb, racism and all the other crap which frightened and depressed them. Frank loved the soft optimism of the song. Later, when he was older, he'd make the song into a challenge. Today he felt like gently caressing the words, like being intimate. Fairy tales can come true, ya see? I did it, so can you. Riddle let Frank's voice do all the work, his strings adding colour and the occasional counterpoint to the voice. Frank liked that a lot.

For the final number of the day (and the year) Frank slipped the narrative into the third person, offering advice on a heartbreaking broad. To himself, it seemed. For Arthur Williams and Carl Sigman's I Could Have Told You sounded like Frank felt. He liked the way the lyrics had him trying to sleep, hearing her making promises she'll never keep. 'And soon it's over and done with, she'll find someone new to have fun with, through all of my tears I could have told you so.' Frank checked that he had his tickets to Spain as he headed out the door.

Swinging with Nelson Riddle.

WRAP YOUR TROUBLES IN DREAMS
1954

WHEN CAPITOL PUT the ten-inch album out in February 1954, they tried hard to sell Songs For Young Lovers to teenagers which, as Frank knew, was never going to work. He'd heard all about some kid in Tennessee called Presley who was stirring up the hicks with some dirty-sounding fast jazz. Frank knew that it was parents who'd buy his record, not least because it was full of cautionary tales. Frank understood people better than those smooth Joes at Capitol. He knew that people loved a fighter, a rebel who had honest old-fashioned values. Frank loved his wife, adored his mother and was always being photographed with his children. Hell, he even had a great relationship with his ex-wife. Against the odds, as ever, Frank knew that he was winning the love of the people. He just had to get over losing the love of the one person who mattered most.

In the middle of February, Frank had his first Top-Ten single hit in five years (the last being The Huckle Buck in 1949). Young At Heart was a smash. It made number two. Songs For Young Lovers made three.

Frank was through with his cockamamie bride. Things were looking up. He was on his way to not having to depend on anyone else, ever again. If his voice went, he wanted to be prepared. That place in the desert was turning into a license to print money. The dough a casino could make! Frank wanted in. It was a bummer that the Feds had to be involved, but he'd gotten a 2 per cent stake in the Sands. In future, he knew that every time someone bought a drink, put a nickel in a machine or threw a dice, he'd be gettin' some of that.

In January he'd agreed to sing a great new Jule Styne and Sammy Cahn number for a Twentieth Century Fox film, Three Coins In A Fountain. They'd paid him $10,000, so on 1 March, he'd also recorded Day In, Day Out again, along with Harold Arlen and Yip Harburg's Last Night When We Were Young. He liked Three Coins, not only because it was written by two old pals, but because it was a neat piece of invention. Like the film it was written for, the song told the tale of three women casting coins into Rome's Trevi fountain, wishing for love, and finding it. Until the record and film release, no-one had ever knowingly thrown coins into the Trevi. A month after, it had to be cleared of money! Frank liked creating legends and myths, it was good for the ego – and for business.

On 25 March Frank felt like the million dollars he knew he was about to make. He and his Oscar took a long walk alone after the Academy Awards, with Frank remembering, recalling and making promises to himself. Those bums who had dismissed him would never have the chance again.

He was the boss now.

He was the only man who told Frank Sinatra what to do. Oscar was his passport to total control, to becoming the Chairman of The Board.

SWING EASY
7, 19 April 1954

FRANK WANTED TO tell the world that he was up again. Songs For Young Lovers was a hit. He'd signed up to do another serious movie, Suddenly, in which he played a hit-man, hired to wipe out the President (and how he wouldn't mind doing that!). And he joined the company of great men – Bogie had initiated him into the Rat Pack, a loose clan of like-minded, hard drinking, outspoken, left-leaning stars. Frank wanted to swing.

Nelson Riddle's vibraphone-led arrangement of Miller, Krueger, Conn and Jule Styne's Sunday was a perfect start. Although the words said Frank was blue all week until meeting his doll, the music and Frank himself were happier than that. Likewise with Cole Porter's Just One Of Those Things, a nonchalant but tight finger-popping swing through a one-night stand. Frank was getting through a few trips to the moon on gossamer wings himself.

For Fred Ahlert and Joe Young's I'm Gonna Sit Right Down And Write Myself A Letter, a clarinet eased Frank into a laid-back, wistful song which had been a hit in the 1930s, and had sounded far more innocent without Riddle's sleazy horns and cool vibes. Frank bent the notes and slurred his pronunciation just enough to add a little dark edge.

Longing for sleep, Frank crooned through Kohler, Moll and Barris's Wrap Your Troubles In Dreams, letting Riddle lighten the middle eight with duelling sax and clarinet. Frank was beginning to believe the song. Castles may crumble, life was funny that way.

Hey, while you got dreams baby, anything was possible. Look at me!

Frank went into the second session for Swing Easy feeling as bright as the Spring flowers bursting around him. He wanted this album to be the day to the night of Songs For Young Lovers. For the fifth time he wanted to do Simon and Marks' All Of Me. Riddle's arrangement sounded like a great live treatment. Frank could feel how the build-up to the final line was perfect for steering a crowd into applause. He didn't feel like imploring anyone to take all of him. No-one was gonna do that again.

Jeepers Creepers by Harry Warren and Johnny Mercer had been a hit for lots of people. Frank liked the song, it was easy to make it work. It swung in the right tempo, fitted with the rest of the tunes for the album.

Get Happy was the one for Frank though. Forget your troubles and just get happy. Yeah man, the sun was shining. Harold Arlen and Ted Koehler hit Frank's spot. Riddle's insistent horns and pacy beat with honking trumpet drove the tune at a great pace. Up, up, up.

It left Frank in the mood for Taking A Chance On Love. He even convinced himself of Duke, Latouche and Fetter's sentiment. Frank really was in the groove again.

IN THE WEE SMALL HOURS OF THE MORNING
February 1955

DAMES. CAN'T LIVE WITH 'EM, can't make a decent record without 'em. Frank had spent most of 1954 shooting Suddenly and Not As A Stranger (with Robert Mitchum), fooling around with the guys, and recording songs for a cartoon version of Finian's Rainbow, which the bums never finished. Ava was always in a different place, with different guys. What else could Frank do? There were always broads around.

He felt kinda lonely though. Dino had Jeannette and loads of company, not that he ever wanted it. Sammy was still pretty shook up by the car crash which took his eye. Frank liked it that Davis had stayed at his Palm Springs place to recuperate.

On 8 February, Frank took pianist Bill Miller into the studio with Nelson Riddle to start work on a new album. Frank planned to sing the blues. He was spending a lot of time living his life at night, rising at Vegas breakfast time (5pm), drinking, joking, playing cards and missing a lover. Dave Mann and Bob Hilliard's In The Wee Small Hours Of The Morning summed up his mood perfectly. Frank had picked sixteen songs this time, not just eight. Capitol had told him they were making twelve-inch discs, onto which he could fit more songs.

In The Wee Small Hours ('that's the time you miss her most of all'), with its symphonic strings and sad lyric, was followed on side one of the record by Duke Ellington's masterly Mood Indigo, Rodgers and Hart's Glad To Be Unhappy, Hoagy Carmichael's I Get Along Without You Very Well, Jimmy Van Heusen and Eddie De Lange's Deep In A Dream, Schwartz and Dietz's I See Your Face Before Me, Swit and James' Can't We Be Friends, and Edgar Swan's When Your Lover Has Gone, which was a far more knowing version than the one Frank recorded with Axel in 1944.

The theme was one of sweet sleep – unreal time when heartaches dull but longing grows. It was a slow descent into loneliness. Frank knew what he was doing, though. Take 'em down, then drag them back up. Make the record an emotional roller-coaster ride. Christ, he was forty this year, he'd loved and lost, and loved some more, and was gonna lose some again, too. These songs were the ones that slowed his live set down and for which he adopted 'the saloon singer', one of his many specially created personas. What was that? Damned if anyone knew. But when Frank said he was a saloon singer everyone believed him. Hell, he believed it.

He'd seen enough drunks slurring sentiment in enough bars to know that in their heads and hearts, these men were pouring out their troubles to bartenders because they had no-one else to talk to. They didn't think anyone else could understand. Well, Frank did. Frank's barroom songs – especially One For My Baby which he'd recorded again last August with some longhair called André Previn on piano for the movie Young At Heart – put into eloquent words what all those lost and lonely drunks were feeling. In The Wee Small Hours was gonna be the album which gathered a whole load of those saloon songs, and took the listener through several shots of bourbon and self-pity, before chucking them out the other side feeling better. Side two of the record kicked in with Cole Porter's smart pondering of the eternal question, What Is This Thing Called Love? Frank didn't care Porter was a fruit, they never bothered him, and he wrote a great lyric. Babes loved it. It had an air of hope about it. Harold Arlen and Yip Harburg's Last Night When We Were Young lent a faintly nostalgic air to the proceedings, urging reminiscences of better times. Alec Wilder's I'll Be Around offered hope and persistence, Arlen and Koehler's Ill Wind showed determination and resistance to meeting the end head-on with a blues trumpet. Rodgers and Hart's It Never Entered My Heart said don't even think about it, while their Dancing On The Ceiling was the most upbeat number on the album. Rather than being about a love lost, it was about a temporary separation, with Frank seeing the image of his chosen one above him. For Malnecks, Signorelli and Gus Kahn's I'll Never Be The Same, Frank pushed closer to the microphone and admits he might have been wrong about things.

Finally, Frank had to say something really personal. This Love Of Mine, written with Hank Sanicola and Sol Parker, was a defiant call to Ava and any other broad that he might fall in love with. Originally recorded in 1941, Frank felt that he had to end In The Wee Small Hours with the line, 'This love of mine, goes on and on'. To anyone listening, Frank knew that the song sounded like a sad but positive statement of undying love. To Ava it was meant to say that he'd get over her. Eventually.

MAKIN' WHOOPEE

1956

FRANK WAS TAKING stock of the last year. In The Wee Small Hours had made number two on the album charts in May. A single, Learnin' The Blues, reached number two the same month. Love And Marriage made number five on the singles chart in November, which was not bad for a song made for TV! He'd recorded it for an NBC teleplay of Our Town, in which he starred alongside Paul Newman and Eve Marie Saint. Hell, its B-side, Another Saturday Night even registered at sixty five. (Love Is) The Tender Trap only made twenty three, but it was out two weeks after Love And Marriage. Capitol had begged him to sign a longer contract, so he agreed to seven. It was his lucky number.

He'd made five films in 1955 – Young At Heart, Not As A Stranger, The Tender Trap, Guys And Dolls and his favourite, Man With The Golden Arm. He hadn't got the part he wanted in On The Waterfront, and lost out to Brando in Guys And Dolls, but he'd sung him off the screen. What a bum that guy was! Mumblin' away, looking for 'motivation' of his character. Look no further than the title, pal! Frank was doing fine – he'd even got an Oscar nomination for Golden Arm.

Striding on and up, Frank formed a production company, Kent Productions, to make films. He'd kicked off with Johnny Concho, starring himself and a bunch of pals including Hank Sanicola and Keenan Wynn. Directed by Don McGuire, the score was the first from Riddle.

Frank had just signed to star alongside Crosby, Grace Kelly and Louis Armstrong in a musical re-make of The Philadelphia Story, using Cole Porter songs. High Society indeed.

Now it was time for another album. After the blues of Wee Small Hours, Frank wanted a swinging collection. Frank felt like celebrating. Hell, things were even good for his friends. Dino had scored a six-week run at number one in the charts with Memories Are Made Of This.

Frank and Grace Kelly on the set of High Society. It was her last movie.

SONGS FOR SWINGING LOVERS

9, 10, 12, 16 January 1956

FRANK HAD TRIED out a bunch of songs at The Sands in December which went down well. As usual Voyle Gilmore and Nelson Riddle were running the technical side of things. Frank felt good, loose and fresh. He even felt young. So the new album kicked off with Josef Myrow and Mack Gordon's You Make Me Feel So Young. It was a masterstroke of planning, and Frank knew it. He presented old tunes like Rubin and Warren's You're Getting To Be A Habit With Me and Burke and Johnston's Pennies From Heaven, with new, high-kicking arrangements making them sound now. The whole collection was zinging with energy and wit. Frank was laughing again. Frank Jr liked to tell a story about how the studio wanted twelve songs, which were duly delivered, but then Capitol decided they wanted three more. The way Jr told it, Frank was called in the middle of the night, and he in turn called Riddle. The next night, Riddle was supposed to have finished sheets on Cole Porter's I've Got You Under My Skin in the back of his car on the way to the session. Apparently after the run-through of this arrangement, the orchestra stood up and cheered, women had tears in their eyes and all that. Frank Jr told a good story, huh? Sure, people in the studio knew something special was happening. Frank felt it most on Frankie Laine and Carl Fischer's We'll Be Together Again. One of the slow songs from the sessions, it was the last cut of the lot, and hung the air with regret that everything must end. But I've Got You Under My Skin had been recorded four days earlier, at the end of a session which included Jones and Kahn's Swingin' Down The Lane and White, Frisch and Wolfson's Flowers Mean Forgiveness, which wasn't actually used on the album, but would be a single.

But hey, Frank knew the value of myth-making in his world.

CLOSE TO YOU
January-November 1956

BEFORE SHOOTING BEGAN on High Society, Frank found himself cuddling up to the mic with Bing Crosby for Well Did You Evah. Frank had to laugh. The song pretty much mirrored the pair's relationship on screen and in life. Crosby respected Frank, and likewise. Alongside the old man, Frank knew he looked and sounded much younger than his forty years.

During the recording Crosby had his way with arrangers, using Skip Martin, so Frank demanded Riddle for his two solo numbers, You're Sensational and Mind If I Make Love To You. Conrad Salinger handled the duet with Celeste Holm, Who Wants To Be A Millionaire.

After filming Society, Frank went back to the studio to make a slow album. He got Riddle to hire the Hollywood String Quartet, to which the arranger added the usual rhythm section and various solo instruments. On 8 March they cut Harold Arlen and Truman Capote's Don't Like Goodbye's, Gordon Jenkins and Johnny Mercer's P.S. I Love You, and Ray Noble and Max Kester's Love Locked Out for the album Close To You. If It's The Last Thing I Do, a Sammy Cahn and Saul Chaplin song, didn't work well enough to make the album. Over 4 and 5 April, Frank cut eight more tunes with the Quartet. Although Riddle wasn't happy with the results, Frank liked the sound. It wasn't as intimate or approachable as Wee Small Hours had been, but it was classy. Just to wind up the Capitol bosses, he snuck in a version of Flaw In My Flue, a ridiculous lyric which compared the object of love with a fireplace. The fatcats at Capitol would probably spit feathers when they heard it. Frank was never gonna put it on Close To You.

While he made more movies in the summer, Capitol compiled This Is Sinatra from early singles sessions. It was to be a Christmas release, which was fine by Frank. He didn't want to rush Close To You, and took 1 November to record the title tune, Hoffman, Livingston and Lampl's Close To You (for the third time), along with Adamson and McHugh's I Couldn't Sleep A Wink Too Much (for the fourth time) and Rodgers and Hart's It's Easy To Remember (for the first time). All of which were nice, gentle warm-ups for the next big album.

Capitol bosses thought Flaw In My Flue was a real song. Frank laughed.

A SWINGIN' AFFAIR
8, 15, 20, 26, 28 November 1956

THE WORLD WAS a rapidly changing place, and Frank seemed to be permanently on the move. He had no fixed base, and for most of 1956 flitted between The Sands, his cottage on the golf course at Palm Springs, New York and Nancy's house in LA. Presley had hit the charts hard, all the kids were getting into Rock'n'Roll. What did they know? They were kids. Plenty of their parents were listening to Frank, looking to him for a lead on what to wear, how to react.

Frank kept on doing what he did best, leading by example. He worked hard, fought with the press, loved his kids, respected his ex-wife, drank with Hollywood's hardest elite (now officially proclaimed the Rat Pack) and dated who he damned well pleased.

One day, someone working with Frank on a movie asked him how he did all the things that he did. Frank didn't blink. 'One thing at a time.'

For five designated days that meant sing and swing, brother. However, the first day set for recording, 8 November, was a waste. Perkins and Parish's Stars Fell On Alabama and the Gershwin brothers' I Got Plenty Of Nuttin' didn't work. Frank had just been voted Musician's Musician by Metronome magazine. He had standards to maintain, whatever the scale of the hangover. The songs were successfully recorded next time out, along with Kern, Fields and McHugh's I Won't Dance, another Astaire number which Frank knew had to be flirtier and dirtier. Frank wanted his Swingin' Affair to be a party hearty record, one which folks could put on to entertain friends, and not help but have a good time. Nelson Riddle's arrangements were jazzy and loudly featured his new trademark, blaring horns.

Frank loved giving tunes he'd grown up with a new treatment. He liked them, so naturally his fans would, too. He would cruise through Cole Porter's You'd Be So Nice To Come Home To, and then bumped against it with Duke Ellington and Paul Webster's I Got It Bad And That Ain't Good, without upsetting the good folks' sense of propriety.

One track recorded at these sessions which Frank just knew was going to become a signature tune, didn't make it onto the finished album. Rodgers and Hart's The Lady Is A Tramp had been a favourite live track for some time, but didn't quite fit the mood of Swingin' Affair, so Frank marked it for the future, as a song that could add to the Sinatra myth. Swingin' Affair had Night And Day as its signature. People get that one. Frank – a man of unavoidable, essential contradictions.

WHERE ARE YOU?
1957

ONE DAY YOU'RE up, the next you're in the dumper. King Rat, Humphrey Bogart, died on 14 January. Capitol's release of Close To You was timely, capturing Frank's mood. The album made number five a month later. In February a newspaper columnist, Dorothy Kilgallen, wrote a six-part exposé of Frank's life. The dumb broad tried to implicate Frank in Mafia activities while insulting him and his family. What could he do? He sent her a tombstone with her name on it. If he really did have pull with made guys, she would've had a real one over her head, right?

Frank tried to tour Australia, but only got as far as Honolulu when the stupid airlines got bookings all screwed up. That cost him $75,000 dollars in no-show fees.

Frank was not happy. Just before filming Pal Joey with Rita Hayworth and Kim Novak, he and Riddle went into the studio to cut two new songs as singles. So Long, My Love by Sammy Cahn and Lew Spence, and Cahn and Tuminello's Crazy Love were, like the session Frank had completed in December, when he recorded Ross Parker's Your Love For Me, and Phil Tuminello's Can I Steal A Little Love?, slated for double-A side release. Can I Steal made nine on the singles chart early in January. The rest of the tracks did not fare so well. Frank liked Riddle, but maybe they both needed a change. Frank decided on a new arranger for the next album.

Gordon Jenkins was a quiet guy who worked well with strings and understated ballads. This suited Frank. Where Are You was to be the soft and low album which always followed a swinging one. It was different from Close To You (which only lasted fourteen weeks on the chart compared to In The Wee Small Hours' twenty nine weeks), with more strings, and was going to be Frank's first album recorded solely in stereo.

As well as Jimmy McHugh and Harold Adamson's title song, Frank chose epic weepies, which Jenkins placed in an early Fall-style musical setting. As Frank finished the last take of day one, Kosma, Prevert and Mercer's Autumn Leaves, he knew that he had a soft session to match Wee Small Hours. Songs such as Green and Heyman's I Cover The Waterfront and Mercer and Raskin's Laura are gentler love songs than the barroom epics of Wee Small Hours, and Jenkins made them sound nice and longing. By the third day of recording, Frank felt strong enough to handle a second version of I'm A Fool To Want You, the song he'd written with Jack Wolf and Joel Heron in 1951, as he and Ava were in the thrall of their love affair.

Now, with her in Spain and ready to cancel their marriage, it seemed right to record it again. Jenkins made the strings bleed like his heart. Frank rode the wave of emotion a little easier than he had done six years earlier. He knew he wouldn't have to record the song again.

Almost blue. Frank lost a good friend in Bogey, and was about to lose his third wife - to a bullfighter.

PAL JOEY and THE JOKER IS WILD
1957

FRANK HAD IDENTIFIED with John O'Hara's anti-hero from the moment he read the book. Rodgers and Hart's Broadway play was good, but to Frank's mind, no stage Pal Joey had been right. The guy was a heel, but he was cool. There was a bit of Frank in Joey. The suits, the Mary-Janes, the hat and Mac, the way with the broads, even the lingo; Frank had it all. Plus, the songs were right. Bewitched was the tender Joey, admitting he'd fallen for the dame. There's A Small Hotel was Joey being sly, seducing the girl into a quiet night together. I Could Write A Book was all confessional charm, with Joey getting almost vulnerable. The Lady Is A Tramp was the one, though. Where Frank was acting Joey for all the other songs, on this one he was himself. It was a big, big tune. Frank was letting the world in on the secret about dames. They liked sex, too! Until now, he'd sung about girls, ladies and love, but this was all about sex, and he figured the world was ready for it. At the Sands he'd been tempted to grind a little to this one. What was it the Presley kid did to upset so many people? Hey, wake up, everybody did it. Sure, some people were gonna be upset about it, but that's OK, it was a film scene Bro, it was Joey Evans giving the lowdown on doing the dirty. Joey was Frank, Frank was Joey. The look, the hard edge of the small-time hustler was linked to Frank from that point on – until he decided to change things again. Frank was never worried that people would ever assume he was the characters he played in movies. He knew that the people would take the attractive parts of the character he was playing and add it to his image, making him more real. Until now he'd been humble and honourable. With Pal Joey, Frank's first big musical lead (which he didn't have to share with Crosby, Kelly, Young or Brando), he added a little underworld edge, but didn't lose the humour. Make 'em laugh and then make 'em cry. Joey was redeemed, because Frank was a good guy.

Just like Joe E Lewis had been in The Joker Is Wild – a much darker, true tale of a singer who got his vocal cords sliced by the Mob, and had to make a comeback telling jokes. That was acting, though. Although it also had a couple of good songs, namely Sammy Cahn and Jimmy Van Heusen's Chicago and All The Way. Those guys were good at getting the mood of songs just right for Frank's movies. There was a lot of Frank in Lewis, too, but Joey was the character that people were gonna love. Frank's hunch was proved right when Chicago only made a measly eighty four on the singles chart in October, although All The Way made fifteen. What a bummer. He hadn't had a Top-Ten for a year, since Hey! Jealous Lover.

Pal Joey, the soundtrack, made two on the album chart in November. Six months earlier A Swingin' Affair had also made number two, with Where Are You making three. Frank couldn't help noticing that the swinging records were staying around the charts longer than the weepies. As soon as he'd finished the Christmas album with Gordon Jenkins (in July already!), and gotten some single stuff out of the way with Riddle, he had to get Billy May on his case.

from the soundtrack of the Columbia Picture

PAL JOEY

An Essex-George Sidney Production

COME FLY WITH ME
October 1957-April 1958

FRANK LIKED WORKING with Nelson Riddle. The guy was unflappable. Frank would call at some ungodly hour after boozing with Dino and Sammy, and say, 'Make the middle eight of tomorrow's first number like Brahms', and sure enough the next day it would sound like Brahms. And if Frank changed his mind and wanted Puccini instead, Riddle would do that. But this Billy May, man, what a difference. Frank was used to working off the cuff, but this was almost madness. The album was a great concept – a musical journey around the world, kicking off with the flight. Frank asked Sammy Cahn and Jimmy Van Heusen to come up with the title track. With its runway-taxiing intro (May had come up with that real late in the day), Come Fly With Me was an instant classic. Frank knew it as soon as Sammy told him about the line 'If you could use, some exotic booze', in place of 'exotic views'.

The three days were a great escape for Frank. His $3 million ABC television show was bombing because bums in grey suits didn't get the joke. How come Dino ad-libbed his way though all those crummy movies, making millions with off-the-cuff jokes, and TV people wanted Frank to rehearse?

He didn't need to, he was in charge, he knew what was funny, and squares learning lines was not. Man, how Jilly Rizzo, Hank and the boys laughed during shooting. So would people at home. Wait for the Christmas special with Crosby, that'd get the ratings.

Frank's mind raced as soon as he left the studio after finishing with May. It looked like he'd have to pull out of his law suit against that crummy magazine Look, for printing filthy lies. He'd had enough of courts anyway. At least the Grand Jury had believed Frank back in July about not busting down that woman's door with Joe DiMaggio last year. Crazy Joe thought Marilyn was inside douching with another broad. Frank drove, that was all. If he'd been in on the raid, they'd sure have got the right room!

Yeah, those travellin' songs – Vernon Duke's Autumn In New York, Grosz and Kennedy's Isle Of Capri, Duke and Harburg's April In Paris, Carroll Coates' London By Night, all topped off by Sammy and Jimmy's Nice To Go Travellin'.

Great songs, swingin' arrangements, great idea. Frank could do with a bit of travelling himself.

At least he had Christmas in the South of France to look forward to, even if he was making a war picture, Kings Go Forth. No singing in the film, but plenty for the broads in the cast and crew. Natalie Wood was a good kid.

Before that, Frank thought about more recordings with Riddle in November and December. Three songs from an old 1947 movie of his, It Happened In Brooklyn, a couple of others and a new favourite slow number which Frank had taken to closing his shows with, Mann, Weiss and Lowe's Put Your Dreams Away (For Another Day). Corny, but cute.

Plus, of course, the TV special with Dino. Ring-a-ding-ding, the Chairman and his lieutenant together on screen. Drinks, jokes, songs and plenty of razzle. It would slay 'em.

THIS IS SINATRA VOLUME TWO
1958

JANUARY, BACK IN LA, and Frank was flying. Come Fly With Me hit Number one. The single Witchcraft hit twenty. The TV show was a hoot, even though people weren't exactly turning on in droves. Too much nightclub shtick, said the critics. What did they know? No time for recordings, which was a shame. A couple of duets with Keely Smith, orchestrated by Billy May in March, but there were no big sessions until May. Betty Bacall was an angel, maybe the two of them should get hitched? Frank liked sunshine in winter, so he went to a place called the Fountainbleu in Miami, where, so many people wanted to be near him, that he broke all records for takings. Sammy pissed Frank off by saying to a reporter that he, Frank Sinatra, should be nicer to people. The bum. Who'd made him laugh when he lost an eye? Who'd told him he'd be as big as ever? Who'd bought him half a pair of binoculars for the good eye, and let him stay at his house in Palm Springs to get away from the press? Now he called all the time to say sorry. He should stop crawling. Dino said Sammy's real sorry. Yeah, so was Frank.

In April Capitol released another This Is Sinatra, made up of stuff recorded the previous March, May, November and December, along with five old singles from 54, 55 and 56. It made eight on the chart, so Frank was happy. It gave him breathing space while he made the new album.

If I Could Sing Like Bing. The Groaner sandwiched by two of his most irreverent fans.

ONLY THE LONELY
5, 29 May, 24, 26 June 1958

IT WAS TIME for a weepy again, this time with Nelson Riddle in charge of arrangements. But for the first time since starting with Capitol, Voyle Gilmore was not producing. Years later he'd tell Sinatra biographer Arnold Shaw, 'As a singer there's no-one like him. As a guy there was no-one more difficult to handle. Each time you saw Frank it was like meeting a different guy. How he treated you depended solely on how he felt at that moment, and what was bugging him.' Frank had a lot to bug him, as Gilmore admitted, so he didn't need a producer who wasn't on top of his job. It didn't look good for Gilmore when, talking to disc jockeys in Chicago, they said they hadn't gotten his latest cuts. Frank figured Gilmore hadn't done the right thing, and had him replaced for the next session by another Capitol producer, Dave Cavanaugh.

Gilmore told Shaw he was relieved. 'Which isn't to say he was a bad guy. Just complex. One time he was acting up, I went at him, "I'm trying pretty hard, Frank," I complained, "and all I get is abuse." He broke into a broad smile. "Don't let anyone get your goat," he said, "not even me." He was so appealing at times he could charm butterflies – and then again, so miserable he could bother a snake.' Cavanaugh decided to be cool, not show fear, and do the best job he could. Frank liked that.

For Only The Lonely, Frank again got Sammy and Jimmy to compose the title song. 'Ya wanna call this For Losers Only?' asked Sammy. 'Yeah,' countered Frank. 'It's for all those losers who drink as hard as they feel.' Frank wanted a weepy record to be as big as In The Wee Small Hours had been. It was time to go back to the barroom. Riddle's slow, spacey arrangements left Frank's voice floating somewhere around the ceiling, dripping pity, longing and love over the words to the eleven great songs, among them Ann Ronnell's Willow Weep For Me (Billie Holiday will love it, thought Frank), Sammy and Jule's Guess I'll Hang My Tears Out To Dry, Haggart and Burke's What's New, and the one truly great number which Frank would record time and time again – seven, in all – Harold Arlen and Johnny Mercer's One For My Baby.

A year after Bogey's death, someone told the press Betty Bacall and Frank were getting married. They split soon after.

In the early 1950s, the nation chased imaginary Commies from under their beds. In 58, Frank met the big Cheese Commie, Khrushchev.

ONE FOR MY BABY
24, 26 June 1958

IT WAS THE third time Frank had recorded the song. And it was the luckiest, he knew that. This was one of those defining moments when Frank understood that he had to be himself, and also be every man who walked into a bar at 2.45am with a heartache the size of the Empire State.

Bill Miller's piano, polished by years of playing the song during Frank's live show, rolled like the sweetest saloon keyboard you ever heard in any half-awake state. On 24 June Frank and Bill did the song without any orchestra. The studio stilled. It was no longer a sterile, working environment.

Frank and Bill turned it into a small, shabby bar in Hoboken for four long, beautiful minutes. Riddle became the bartender to whom Frank said 'make the music easy and sad'. Two days later, the orchestra did just that, barely intruding on the lonely reverie. It was probably one of the greatest recordings Frank ever made. A week later the last remaining physical reminder of Ava, her Barefoot Contessa statue, was taken away from Frank's drive.

When Only The Lonely was released in September, it went straight to Number one in the LP charts. It stayed in the Top Forty for more than two years. Sure, Frank loved the record.

COME DANCE WITH ME
9, 11, 22, 23 December 1958

SAMMY AND JIMMY did it again. Frank wanted another swinging concept. Dancing. That was it. Billy May would make the tunes swing in a fast tempo, Frank put together a bunch of songs which involved dancing. Sammy Cahn and Jimmy Van Heusen had to open and close the record. Come Dance With Me was 'easy' proclaimed Sammy. He just mixed The Clan lingo ('Come on toots, put on your dancing boots') with Jimmy's upbeat tune. How to close it, though? Simple, there had never been a Last Dance. It was the smoochy end of a Prom/dinner-dance number during which love was pledged and arrangements for future dates made, along with mental notes never to do it again. In between came Irving Berlin's I Could Have Danced All Night and Cheek To Cheek (Astaire tipped over again), Schwartz and Dietz's Dancing In The Dark, Johnny Mercer's Something's Gotta Give, Rube Bloom and Johnny Mercer's Day In, Day Out, Jerome Kern and Oscar Hammerstein's Baubles, Bangles And Beads and four other cool tunes.

Once again, the concept was great and the execution had been good. Leading up to Christmas the sessions had seemed like party night at The Sands with Joey Bishop, Sammy, Betty Bacall, Shirley MacLaine and Dino (with both of whom Frank had just been seen in the very serious soapy movie, Some Came Running) all dropping by for jokes, drinks and chats. When was Frank sleeping? Who needed sleep?

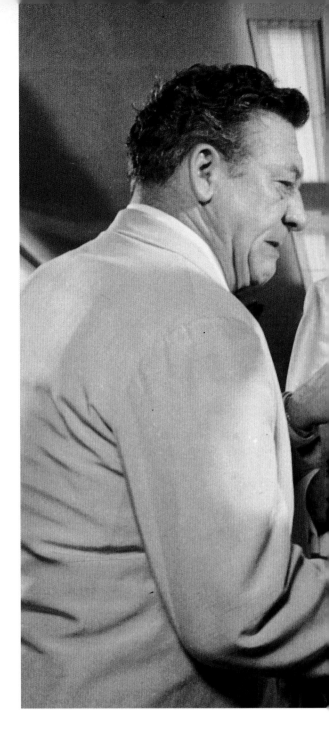

LOOK TO YOUR HEART
1959

IN JANUARY AGAIN, as the previous year, Frank scored a big hit album – although Come Dance With Me didn't make number one, it would stay around the charts for almost twice as long as Come Fly With Me. Capitol Records, which had been small-time when Frank signed with them, had grown, mostly on the back of his success and that of his pals. In the last year Dino

Ain't that a Hole In The Head. The film High Hopes gave Frank a hit, and some pretty good reviews for the acting.

had hit big with singles like Return To Me, Buone Serra, Rio Bravo, Sleepy Time Gal and All I Do Is Dream Of You.

Even the compilation records Capitol were putting out made the Top Ten – Look To Your Heart made eight in May 1959. Didn't everyone have that stuff on single? Frank was walking past Capitol Tower's new office on Vine Street one day with Mo Ostin, a smart cookie who knew the music business. Frank suddenly announced that he wanted his own label. Mo said 'Why not?' So Frank put

his lawyers on it, promising Mo the post of chief exec.

Things were shaping up well, Frank hoped to be his own boss pretty soon. Meanwhile, he had to keep making records. Not just for the money, but because he really dug it. The films were OK, but the shows, and records, they were the gasser. Vegas was becoming the Clan's own playground. On 28 January, Frank and Dag (short for dago, as they called each other) played their first proper show together at The Sands. The people loved it. Frank sang, Dag clowned, then they did some numbers together. Man, what a thrill, and what a party after.

NO ONE CARES
24, 25, 26 March, 14 May 1959

EARLIER IN MARCH the great Billie Holiday had told her manager that she wanted to make an album like Frank's Only The Lonely. Frank was humbled. He wanted to make a blues album that Billie would love. Gordon Jenkins was hired again; it was weepy time. Sammy and Jimmy excelled themselves with the title tune. Frank even convinced himself that no-one cared and his phone never rang. His voice was gentle yet strong – the boyish, higher register of early recordings was gone, replaced with a grown man's rich tenor. Jenkins' arrangements were stately, almost funereal, the strings in minor keys, humming in the background with a perceptible sadness. Frank almost sobbed the last lines of Willard Robinson and Larry Conley's A Cottage For Sale, as the violins edged lower and lower along their scale. Arlen and Koehler's Stormy Weather, an old favourite of Frank's, was positively mournful – and not completely successful because of that. But it set the tone for a swelling, deeply romantic, almost hymn-like Where Do You Go, by Alec Wilder. By the time Victor Young, Bing Crosby and Ned Washington's A Ghost Of A Chance swooned in, the unrelenting mood of despair was almost suffocating. Frank Jr once called Only The Lonely 'like death'. He can't have had words for No One Cares. Ghost was the most upbeat things got on the disc.

Johnny Burke and Jimmy Van Heusen's Here's That Rainy Day brought side one to a gloomy close. Nobody could possibly hear those six songs without thinking; Frank's suffered. Where did the inspiration for these and the last six heartbreaking performances came from? Maybe Frank was thinking of Ava again. The crazy dame was in Australia when he was, during April. It was fun, but not earth-shattering.

Frank recorded the title track, plua, for the fifth time, Ruth Lowe's I'll Never Smile Again on 14 May, back in Hollywood using Nelson Riddle as conductor (but with Jenkins' arrangements). Frank thought of Tommy Dorsey, not Ava, as he crooned through the song which was a standard for him back in the early 1940s. Maybe fans thought of early Frank too, when they heard the album. It sold as well as anything he'd done back then, and made number two on the charts in August.

HIGH HOPES
Summer, Fall 1959

MAN, THESE MOVIES weren't no fun no more. Sure, Hole In The Head opened with rave reviews – for Frank's songs, All My Tomorrows and High Hopes (almost a goddamn novelty record, if you asked Frank, what with all those kids yelping away. What was Sammy Cahn doin' to him?). In it, Frank played a bad single dad who wanted to turn a crummy Miami hotel into the Hilton. His bro, Edward G Robinson, would only lend Frank the money if his son went to NY to live with Ed G. Making it was a bummer. When would these guys dig that Frank was an instinctive actor? He couldn't rehearse, he'd lose the edge. Likewise the war flick, Never So Few. At least on that he got to 'work' with Peter Lawford. What a big-league broad chaser that guy was. McQueen was a pain, though. The boy should lighten up. Frank wanted to work with pals, only, from now on. Like with the record company thing, Frank wanted to be Pope. Can Can looked like fun, Shirley MacLaine the mouse was in it, so was a gasser of a chick, Juliet Prowse. Legs foreversville. In the middle of making the French-style movie, Russian President Kruschev and his wife visited the set. That right-wing prig Reagan refused to show, but Rita Hayworth and Gregory Peck made it. Frank did the honours, chatted with Kruschev's dame about kids, and sang C'est Magnifique for them. Politics was fun, huh?

The only sessions to take place for the rest of the year are in September and October for Can Can. Duets with Shirley MacLaine (Cole Porter's Let's Do It), Maurice Chevalier (Porter's I Love Paris and Montmart), and solo shots at Porter's C'est Magnifique and It's All Right With Me. Riddle was as dependable as ever. They made plans for the next album.

NICE 'N' EASY
March 1960

FRANK HAD A new love. Juliet Prowse was almost as tough as Ava, and just as contrary. Breaking with the routine of the past five years, Frank decided that he wanted to record a ballad album. For the first three days of March, he sang some old favourites. Coots and Gillespie's You Go To My Head, Mercer and Bloom's Fools Rush In, Brown and Fain's That Old Feeling and Woods, Campbell and Connolly's Try A Little Tenderness were all songs Frank had recorded between 1945 and 1950, mostly with Axel Stordahl. He was 44, and getting a little tired. He and the Summit (as the Clan became) had just filmed Ocean's Eleven in Vegas. That's Frank, Dag, Smokey (Sammy Davis Jr), Peter Lawford, Joey Bishop, Richard Conte and Henry Silva in Vegas, making a movie. When did Frank sleep? Between eight and five in the day naturally, when in the desert. But this was film time, not showtime, so they worked then. And then they went and played. And after the filming, Frank made a TV special with Juliet. Sometime around when, Joe Kennedy, an old-time bootlegger but now father of wannabe Democratic nominee John F, and father-in-law to Peter Lawford, asked Frank for help getting Jack nominated. Frank said sure, he'd talk to Sam. Giancana was asked as a personal favour to Frank to mobilise West Virginia local sheriffs and unions and deliver 120,000 votes in Jack's favour. Sam sent Skinny, who'd had Frank play eight sell-out shows at the 500 Club last July and owed him big anyway. The Chairman and the Summit campaigned across the country for Kennedy. No wonder Frank wanted to take it Nice 'N' Easy.

It was a new outlook for him, and for America. Frank wanted to show that he could kick back, relax and be a pal. For the sleeve he wore a cardigan, for Chrissakes. Everyone remembered the old songs, and how good they could still be. The mood of nostalgia harked back to the days when America won the war and the world looked brighter. That time when the future looked so inviting. 'Hey,' said Frank on Nice 'N' Easy, 'it still is!' The album distanced Frank from the Vegas nights, and put him back in the afternoon schedule for the little lady at home.

The title track came to him while he campaigned for JFK. He recorded Spence, Keith and Spencer's Nice 'N' Easy at the beginning of a session on 13 April.

The month after JFK won his party's nomination – Frank sang The Star Spangled Banner at the convention in LA. Nice 'N' Easy hit the number one spot. Frank liked politics. Up close it was attractive, the power was sexy. Being Number One meant everything to him, just as it clearly did to JFK. Frank checked how his new company was coming along. He figured there were only two more albums for Capitol.

SWINGIN' SESSION!
22, 23 August 1960

TIME TO SWING, but with an innocence. No more Pal Joey. Nelson Riddle made the arrangements as upbeat and happy as possible. Frank wanted to kick the album off with the number that made Danny Wilson so sweet for him; Shay, Fisher and Goodwin's When You're Smiling. And he wanted it at pace. Riddle had to double up all the tempos. Since getting the highest TV rating ever for his Welcome Home Elvis special in March, Frank had developed a liking for some Rock'n'Roll. So Rodgers and Hart's Blue Moon got a snappy treatment. As did Walter Donaldson and George Whiting's My Blue Heaven, which Frank had covered ten years earlier. It was this version which was to become the seminal one, though. Fresh, finger-popping, it was like a live, nightclub performance which thundered along without totally losing its innocent intent. Frank, though, sounded as if he'd got a sneer on his face, while the band kicked through it so fast they sounded as if they wanted to get to their own personal blue heavens. Every other track is run through as fast, and the album became the shortest Frank ever released. He was in a hurry. Not only did he have to get out of the Capitol contract, but he had a business to buy. Frank, along with Dag, Hank and Skinny, applied to take over the Cal-Neva Lodge, a casino at Lake Tahoe. He also had to give Nancy Jr away to singer Tommy Sands in Vegas, on 11 September. So on 31 August, and 1 September, Frank finished Swingin' Session! and laid down a mad, frantic and almost lewd version of Ol' Macdonald, adapted by Lew Spence, Marilyn Keith and Alan Bergman (the farmer had a lot of chicks). Swingin' Session! would make three on the album chart in February 1961. Two months later the compilation All The Way, which included High Hopes, Ol' Macdonald and All The Way, made number four.

POINT OF NO RETURN
December 1960-September 1961

FRANK WOULD GO back into the studio before the end of 1960. Not for Capitol, but for himself. His company, Reprise, had been formed, and was about to start trading, as soon as Frank had a record to release. Needless to say, the bums at Capitol weren't happy. He still owed them. There was nothing he could do, but make two more albums for them, plus a single. In March 1961 Frank got together with Billy May once more for another themed album. The best Frank could manage was Come Swing With Me. May wanted a bigger than usual band, which was fine by Frank as Capitol were paying. Both men decided that a look back at the big-band days was a good idea, so would choose songs to fit. Heinie Beau was brought in to give some tunes an authentic feel – Brown, Homer and Green's Sentimental Journey and Fields and McHugh's On The Sunny Side Of The Street could almost be Tommy Dorsey, while Evans, David and Altman's American Beauty Rose was handled far better by Heinie and May than Mitch Miller ever managed. Billy May did a great Harry James-style job on Sammy Cahn and Jule Styne's I've Heard The Song Before. The record would make eight on the chart in August of 1961. Frank's final whole album session for the company which had taken a chance on him when he needed a break saw him reunited with the man who helped take him to Capitol. Axel Stordahl was back in LA. He was unwell, suffering from cancer, but was still a hell of an arranger as far as Frank was concerned. So over two days in early Fall 1961 (11 and 12 September), Axel conducted the orchestra for Frank's last album session for Capitol (Skip Martin would handle the single recording of I Gotta Right To Sing The Blues on 6 March, 1962). The choice of songs was as poignant as ever, with Frank re-recording Kurt Weill and Maxwell Anderson's September Song with some meaning. When he and Axel first recorded it, Frank was only thirty one. Fifteen years later, the singer was closer to his September years. There was a lot of reminiscing between the two old friends. They re-recorded Strachey, Link and Marvell's These Foolish Things, and wallowed in nostalgia with Herman Hupfield's As Time Goes By, and Reye, DePaul and Johnston's I'll Remember April. They finally said goodbye on the record with Blake and Razaf's Memories Of You. Point Of No Return wouldn't be released until April 1962 (it made nineteen in the chart), by which time Axel was very ill. Frank was singing to no-one except Axel in those sessions. He wasn't in love with the guy like he loved dames, but he did love him like a big brother. He was going to miss him.

As a new decade began, Frank made another beginning. As the President's man, he arranged and conducted JFK's inaugural gala in 1961. Here he runs an all-star chorus through a number. (L-R) Nat King Cole, Harry Belafonte, Kay Thompson, Jimmy Durante, Helen Traubel, Sammy Kahn, unidentified, Gene Kelly, Janet Leigh, Peter Lawford, Milton Berle.

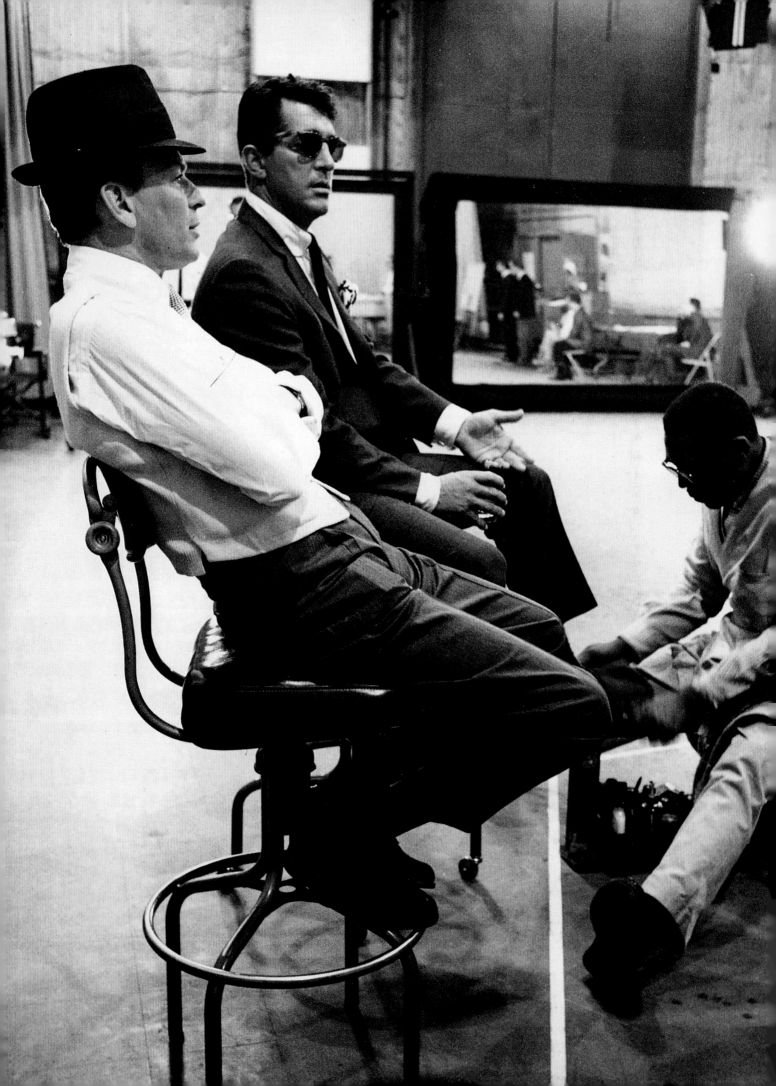

THE REPRISE YEARS

RING-A-DING-DING
19-21 December 1960

FRANK LOOKED AROUND the studio. These guys had better be good. He was paying for them, they were going to help him create the first record for his new company. He couldn't get Riddle (because of those Capitol bums holding him to his contract) or May, but Frank remembered a trombone player who'd given Tommy Dorsey a run for his solos – Johnny Mandel, who also happened to be a fair jazz arranger. Frank had dug his score to Susan Hayward's film I Want To Live. Frank had asked Sammy Cahn and Jimmy Van Heusen to write the first number and the title of the record. But, as usual, Frank had given them the title: Ring-A-Ding-Ding. It was Clan philosophy, pure and simple.

On the surface at least, Frank was on top of the world, everything was ring-a-ding-ding. He was America's undisputed champion singer, the President of the United States wanted to be his pal, the most beautiful women in the world wanted to have his children, he ran Vegas and had Hollywood on the back foot. No-one told him what to do.

Except, except … it wasn't all smooth going. Capitol records were trying hard to piss him off by planning releases at the same time his new stuff would come out on Reprise. At least Mo Ostin reckoned it didn't matter – he said people wanted whatever Frank Sinatra did.

And JFK was acting a bit funny lately. That damned brother of his, the square, Catholic-wedded Robert, didn't like Frank and his Clan. Since a lot of what Bobby said went for Jack, Frank had publicly denounced the idea of the Clan back in August. Sammy Davis, for whom Frank was best man at his wedding to Swedish bombshell May Britt on 13 November, had been taken off the appearance list for the inaugural gala Frank was arranging on Bobby's orders, because of the 'racially sensitive' nature of his marriage. JFK was now king of Camelot, his brother

didn't want him embarrassed.

On the face of it, Frank was the Pope. But, as he stood in the studio at the dawn of yet another new beginning, during studio time which he was paying for again (but which at least he could now afford), Frank felt tired and a touch irritable. Mandel had arranged a bunch of classic nightclub numbers for him in a hard-edged, swinging style, like they were made for The Sands. Frank sighed. He was forty-five for Chrissakes. OK, he thought, let's go for it. Let's kick off with Ring-A-Ding-Ding, to remind us of what it's all about. No, he didn't need no rehearsal. Who had time?

A snare roll into a band of honking horns and ringing bells, eight bars and then Frank: 'Life is dull, it's nothin' but one big lull, then presto you do a skull, and find you're reeling, chastising your feelings, like a toy on a string and your heart's going ring-a-ding-ding, ring-a-ding-ding'.

It was a hymn to the unexpected, a call to let anything happen, be yourself, fall in love on sight. It was almost a re-write of Anything Goes, and there was nothing wrong with that. In truth it was not a great song. Frank knew it, but what else could he do? He had to make the damned record, he couldn't let Capitol have all his fans to themselves next year.

Harold Arlen and Ted Koehler's Let's Fall In Love lifted Frank a bit. It was familiar territory, he loved the song. Likewise Cole Porter's In The Still Of The Night. But the Gershwin's A Foggy Day

dragged a bit. It wasn't on the money, the band were too showtime, they didn't have enough class.

The next day things weren't much better. Irving Berlin's Let's Face The Music And Dance just didn't glide, while Cole Porter's You'd Be So Easy To Love was just about OK, with Frank struggling to hit the right notes at the right time. He managed to saunter through Kern and Fields' medium paced A Fine Romance, before Mandel got the band swinging for The Coffee Song. At least that felt like old times. Skip Martin came in with the arrangement for Irving Berlin's Be Careful It's My Heart, but Frank could only occasionally catch the right tone. He was in key, but felt like he was coming down with a cold or something. Rodgers and Hart's Have You Met Miss Jones was so bad Frank didn't want to keep a take.

The next day Mandel ran through a Dick Reynolds' arrangement of Berlin's I've Got My Love To Keep Me Warm. Frank thought of Dag and eased back from the crooning. James Hanley's Zing! Went The Strings Of My Heart was better. Frank felt at home with what had become a live favourite. He still couldn't ram the notes home, though (that master would have to be lost). Schwartz and Dietz's You And The Night And The Music had a nice, modern feel to the orchestration, but Frank just couldn't make it happen. It was an OK take, but not really up enough. Why he'd agreed to do Fain, Kahal and Norman's When I Take My Sugar To Tea, he didn't know. Man, it was a relief to hand the baton over to Felix Slatkin. He conducted Nelson Riddle arrangements of Sammy and Jimmy's The Last Dance, The Second Time Around and Tina. The last two were going to be his first Reprise single. It was amazing the effect Riddle's arrangements had on Frank. Even though it was the end of a long, mostly unsatisfactory session, he found his true voice for the last three numbers. Maybe it was because the horns were working with him, not battling against him.

Elvis is back – Frank welcoming him on his return from the Army, live on ABC TV.

THE PRESIDENT'S MEN

6-20 January 1961

AS FRANK STEPPED down from the Caroline, JFK's private plane, snow was gently falling on Washington. At least it kept the press away from the Lincoln the White House had sent to pick up Frank, Peter Lawford and the $90,000 worth of cigarette boxes that Frank had brought from Rusar's in Beverley Hills. They were real silver, inscribed and destined for all the stars who'd heeded Frank's call to appear at the JFK's Inaugural Gala: compere Joey Bishop, conductor Bernstein, Belafonte, Milt Berle, Nat King Cole, Mahalia Jackson, Tony Curtis and Janet Leigh, Bette Davis, his own sweet Juliet, even Eleanor Roosevelt. Frank made a note to confirm that he'd bought up all the tickets to Becket on Broadway for the 19th – that was one sure way to make sure that Laurence Olivier would also be there. This was gonna be a blast.

At the National Guard Armoury the press started asking dumb questions about Frank's friends. Some schmuck brought up Albert Maltz again. What was with these guys? Frank had backed off from using the blacklisted Commie writer, hadn't he? It stank that those Hollywood studios would hire Trumbo, Young and even Maltz at cheap rates to write under a different name. Goddamned hypocrites. Joe Kennedy had told Frank to drop Maltz, or be dropped from Jack's campaign. He wasn't gonna let those bums tell him what to do. They had even started in on his suit! Frank had Hollywood designer Don Loper run off two identical sets of evening wear. Some smartass thought Loper only made dresses.

What the hell. Now he understood why Dag had stayed away. Here he was, appointed by the President-elect himself to organise what would be the biggest night of the year.

The weekend before the ball, Frank made an appearance on Leland Hayward's TV special, The Gershwin Years. It was the only way he could get Ethel Merman for the gala. He duetted with her on Let's Call The Whole Thing Off and ran through I've Got A Crush On You, A Foggy Day (which was much better than it had been last month) and Nice Work If You Can Get It. Frank was tired, and it showed. He was also planning a tribute show at Carnegie Hall for Martin Luther King, for which Dino and Sammy were coming to New York. Frank figured it was a fitting smack in the mouth to the square-head schmucks who hadn't wanted his pals at the President's big night.

The ball itself was a gasser. Snowdrifts in the streets kept plenty of people away, but the important guys were there. After the show, right there on stage, the President personally thanked Frank for all he'd done. Man, that made Frank so proud. He was glad he'd recorded everything, it'd make a great album for Reprise.

The next night, Frank held a private party for all the stars who'd trudged through the snow to make the event. Jack was downstairs at the Statler Hilton with Jackie (who Frank figured didn't like him much), LBJ and Mrs LBJ. Frank was downing Jack Daniels and water with Juliet, kicking back, when JFK suddenly loomed over the table. And he was apologising to Frank for busting in! Now that was class. After a few more drinks with Frank and that crazy opera dame Callas, JFK was dragged back to Squaresville and his little wife. It had been a good few weeks for Frank. But somehow he knew it wouldn't stay that way.

Frank was beginning to wonder about these other Kennedys. Not wanting Sammy around he could just about get a handle on. But why had Bobby ordered all pictures of Frank and JFK to be taken away from Frank? Why was it that Frank was not allowed to brag about the wild nights he and Jack and had enjoyed last year at Frank's place in Palm Springs? Maybe Sam Giancana was right about them. Sam was working out a plan with the CIA to whack Castro, but kept complaining about Bobby's boys tapping his phone, shaking him down. Frank told Sam he'd do him a favour, talk to the Prez, get his little brother off Sam's case. Somehow though, Frank didn't think Jack was listening.

REMEMBERING TOMMY
20-22 March, 1-3 May 1961

CAPITOL HAD PUSHED Sinatra's Swingin' Session to number three in the LP charts. They'd just released All The Way (which would make four), and had a cut-price collection of Frank's early albums planned for release. Mo couldn't get Ring-A-Ding-Ding out until May and anyway Frank wasn't over the moon about the way the record turned out. He knew he needed another big album like Come Fly With Me. So while he worked with Billy May for the three-day Come Swing With Me session paid for by Capitol, he arranged to run through some numbers with Sy Oliver, an old friend from Dorsey days. Although none of the numbers were mastered, it was a valuable exercise for Frank. He and Sy had wanted to do a tribute album to their former mentor (Sy had arranged for Tommy when Frank sang with the band) and Frank needed, in the words of Bassman and Washington's song, 'to get sentimental over something'.

Business work was harder than filming and recording. Sam Giancana was on at Frank to get Kennedy's Feds called off, and to whack Desi Arnez, whose Untouchables TV show was showing a lot of disrespect to his pals (Sam had driven for Al Capone in the early days). Joey Fischetti, an old pal from Hoboken and cousin to Al Capone, had also called, telling Frank to straighten the Cuban out. What did he expect Frank to do? In the end, Frank pulled out of a deal with Arnez involving storage space for Frank's production company, Kent. He also tried talking to the little runt, but he always had those bodyguards around him.

So, at the end of swinging sessions with Billy May, Frank was enjoying run-throughs of favourite Dorsey numbers like I'm Getting Sentimental Over You; Meyer, Adams and Baer's There Are Such Things; Van Heusen and Burke's Polka Dots And Moonbeams; Fain and Kahal's I'll Be Seeing You. He and Sy went through eight numbers in two nights. By the time Frank put the songs on tape in May, he'd added four more; Bowman's East Of The Sun, West Of The Moon, Grofe

and Adamson's Daybreak, Kahn and Jones' The One I Love Belongs To Somebody Else, and Fischer and Carey's It Started All Over Again. Frank loved the record, he thought it was the best thing he'd done in years. His voice was in the best shape it had been in since last December. It made Frank feel young again and strong. The recording of I Remember Tommy went so well that he immediately booked Billy May and his orchestra for a modern, swinging album session two weeks later.

SINATRA SWINGS
17, 18, 19, 23 May 1961

FRANK WAS BACK in full swing, and he wanted the world to know it. He was in the middle of making Sergeants Three with the whole Clan and man, what a time they were having. Instead of the long nights wiping him out, Frank felt energised by it all. Even director John Sturges was in on the fun. Ring-A-Ding-Ding made number six on the album chart. Frank was in regular contact with JFK, who it seemed to Frank wanted to join the Clan. His little Nancy was making records for Reprise, and even had minor hits in Italy and Japan. Frank picked out a bunch of new (to him) songs which had the right feel. Gus Khan and Ted Fiorito's I Never Knew positively zinged. Billy May's horns were hard, just the right side of harsh as they drove the melody along. Frank really dug the double bass up close to his voice.

Benny Goodman, Edgar Sampson and Mitchell Parish's Don't Be That Way started out as laid back as Ella liked to do it, but built smoothly to a fierce middle-eight. Joe Marsala's Don't Cry Joe was on the slow side and lacked any self-pity the way Frank saw it. The song was a man-to-man piece of advice about a broad. This was sophistication at a time when the singles charts were full of pap songs, novelty records and kids demanding attention. Frank knew his audience was above all that. The most powerful man in the Western world put his records on when he had important people over to the White House. Not Elvis Presley's or Eddie Fisher's or, God forbid, Lawrence Welk's.

The Chairman and the Prez. JFK wanted to be in Frank's gang. Bobby Kennedy ordered all pics of the men partying to be destroyed.

Eddie Fisher
looking pained as
the Clan take over
his Coconut Grove
opening night.
Dino told him
he should be at
home with wife
Elizabeth Taylor.

... AND STRINGS

July-November 1961

CAPITOL HAD STOPPED Frank calling his Reprise album with Billy May Swing Along With Me. So he responded by re-titling it Sinatra Swings and rushed to put it out in the same week as Capitol's Come Swing With Me. The Reprise album sold better (not by much, but at least it was something). On 10 July Frank, Smokey and Judy Garland – who was looking kind of rough these days – performed for the Democrats at their Beverley Hills Hotel Convention. Frank sat with the Prez. On 25 July, Frank finally had his revenge on Eddie Fisher. It was Fisher's opening night at the Coconut Grove, and Elizabeth Taylor's first night out since she had almost died from pneumonia. As the whole Clan took their seats, the audience turned from Fisher's opening number to watch. When the singer on stage reached the middle of That Face, Dino yelled out, 'If I were you, I wouldn't be working, I'd be home with her.' The audience broke up. Frank laughed. Ten minutes later, bored with the crooners' square treatments of fine songs, he led Dag, Smokey and Joey Bishop onto the stage, splashing JD everywhere. The stage was theirs for the next twenty minutes. The paying customers got a whole better ticket than they dreamed of. Fisher sat at the side of the stage while the pros entertained. Later Fisher said he had known what was coming. Sure you had, pal.

In August Frank and Dino flew to London to make a guest appearance in the last Hope and Crosby Road movie, which proved a tired flick, before flying to Germany to make a few bucks. Back in 'Vada in late August, Frank took his share of The Sands to 9 per cent. Then he, Hank and Sanford Waterman formed Park Lake Enterprises and bought Cal-Neva. Frank liked Tahoe, and loved running a club.

In September, Frank spent a weekend with the Kennedy clan at their East Coast holiday camp, Hyannisport. Again, the Prez sent Caroline, his plane, to pick up Frank, Peter Lawford, Ted Kennedy and Porfirio Rubirosa (one-time Dominican Ambassador) and his latest wife. They sailed a bit, drank a lot, and Frank sang some. Over the weekend Lawford tried to get Bobby to listen to Frank about calling the Feds offa Giancana. As usual Bobby was not listening. Jack did hear Frank out about a new movie, however, that he wanted to make. The Manchurian Candidate, based on Richard Condon's novel, was a psychologically disturbing story about a President's assassination, as ordered by the secret service. UA, Frank's distributors, didn't want him to make the picture. So Frank asked Jack to tell them it was OK. JFK liked the book, and told Frank to make it as he would like to see it.

What a life.

Early in November, Frank got a call from Jack Entratter, the manager of The Sands. Sammy Davis was going over-schedule in his act, which stopped people getting to the tables. Could Frank help? On 4 November, Frank walked on stage as Sammy was singing, got his bodyguards to pick him up and carried him off. Sammy got the hint.

That night at 2.30am Frank ran through his set with Tony Morelli and the orchestra. Using charts from his last few recordings, Frank plotted a set which could be recorded live. He'd just signed Dino away from Capitol, and had also taken on saxophonist Ben Webster and singer Jimmy Witherspoon among others – however the label needed another big Sinatra hit. Unfortunately Morelli was no Riddle or May. The show was fine, but couldn't go out. Frank booked the studio for an album of ballads. He'd try some strings again, this time with a new arranger, Don Costa. The kid had done good work with Eydie Gorme, and brought Trini Lopez to Frank at Reprise. Frank liked his arrangements for what would be a Top-Ten ballad album. Stand-out track for Frank was Arlen and Mercer's Come Rain Or Come Shine, which featured a muted trumpet counterpoint to his weary, determined vocal. The strings swelled, a harp trickled and the bass walked Frank's vocal through a sublime lyric. The final verse, played big and bold, would be one Frank would use in live shows. This version would be the way everyone from then on would play the number. Kern and Harbach's Yesterdays was hard to do, yet Frank found the offbeat cellos warm and the French horns a piece of genius. For Hoagy Carmichael's Stardust, Frank focused on Mitchell Parish's often forgotten verse instead of the chorus. It was a great session.

ALL ALONE
January 1962

FRANK AND JULIE, although dating other people, got a crazy idea to become engaged. Frank did the asking, on the agreement that she'd give up film work and be his wife. The only time he'd really been happy in a relationship was when Nancy stayed home and had kids. He liked Julie's spirit, though. For the hell of it, Frank told the press he was 46, and it was time he settled down. Maybe he really felt it. An old pal, comedian Ernie Kovacs had just passed away.

Frank was kind of glad that he'd booked Gordon Jenkins for a recording session on 15 January – it was the day of Ernie's funeral and Frank had been a pallbearer. As Frank stood in the studio, shoulders hunched, hands in pockets, leaning into the microphone, the tears that wouldn't come at the funeral found an escape in his voice. The song sure had ended for Ernie, but the melody lingered on. It was the only time he'd record Berlin's All Alone. For the beginning of the song, Frank wanted a naked first two lines. The strings, as ever with Jenkins, hung back, allowing Frank to feel as blue as the song demanded. The session was completed with Rapee and Pollack's Charmaine, which was not a total success, and another Berlin song, When I Lost You. For the next two days, Frank wallowed in his blue mood. At the end of the third day, after an idling attempt at a song Presley had made his own, Turk and Handman's Are You Lonesome Tonight, Frank couldn't get into Jimmy Van Heusen and Sammy Cahn's specially commissioned Come Waltz With Me – even though he wanted the record to use it as a title. All Alone had already, to Frank's mind, become the lead track.

Some good news reached Frank as he wrapped up the sessions. JFK was coming to Palm Springs with the whole shooting match, and wanted to stay with Frank. At last, public recognition of how close they were. Frank set about building a helipad and extra guest bungalows at the house. Then he started on The Manchurian Candidate.

Dino, Sammy and Frank relaxing after the Martin Luther King benefit at Carnegie Hall a week after JFK's inaugural ball, to which Dag and Smokey weren't invited.

DON'T 'CHA GO 'WAY MAD
February-April 1962

ST VALENTINE'S DAY, for their engagement party, Frank and Julie were guests of honour at Mad Emperor Romanoff's place in Beverley Hills. Frank smiled through clenched teeth. Julie was refusing to give up work. As they climbed the steps to the door, Frank told her 'films or me', and gave her a diamond ring. She didn't answer. A week later, Juliet signed a new deal with Twentieth Century Fox and Frank signed them off as a couple. It was not a good month for the Leader, as Dag and Smokey called him. On returning to Palm Springs to prepare for the Prez, Frank had a call from Peter Lawford. He and Frank were not on best terms at that moment. Frank had asked for too much money to appear in a Lawford film production (The Great Train Robbery), and in December they'd dissolved a partner arrangement for owning a restaurant. Lawford apologised, but ... 'that sonofabitch Bobby had told Jack he couldn't stay with Frank, because he'd be sleeping in a bed that known gangsters – Sam Giancana, Joey Fischetti, Skinny D'Amato – had slept in.' Bobby (with Jackie's full approval) made it clear to Jack that the love affair with Frank's Clan was over. Bobby had reports from the FBI detailing phone taps on Frank's Chicago buddies, in which Sinatra was mentioned over and over again. In a cruel twist of the knife, Bobby told Jack to stay at Bing Crosby's house, and pretend to Frank it was because his place was open on all sides, while Crosby's backed on to a mountain. 'Crosby's a fuckin' Republican,' yelled Frank. He slammed the phone down and ran outside to where the helipad had just been built. Grabbing a sledge-hammer, Frank took out all his frustrations on the smooth concrete.

The weekend the Prez arrived in Palm Springs, Frank flew to Vegas.

The next month, on 10 April, Frank took Neal Hefti – a new arranger who knew his way around a big band, and was held in high regard by soloists – into the studio with a massive brass-led orchestra for a swinging album session. Frank had tried the guy out for two sides at the end of February (Koehler and Bloom's Everybody's Twistin', a blatant attempt to cash in on the craze sweeping America, and Nothing But The Best). Hefti worked on ten of the songs, all standard Sinatra fare, from Cole Porter's I Get A Kick Out Of You and the Gershwin's They Can't Take That Away From Me, to Harry Warren and Mack Gordon's Serenade In Blue and Schertzinger and Mercer's Tangerine. Frank liked the idea of doing Mercer and Malneck's Goody Goody – a recent live favourite – with five trombones, five saxes and four rhythm men. He also added Mundy, Stillman and Jacquet's Don'Cha Go 'Way Mad. Swinging Brass indeed.

The face of experience. A Reprise press shot.

GREAT SONGS FROM GREAT BRITAIN (AND FRANCE)
April-June 1962

HAVING GOT OVER being mad about being kicked out of Camelot, Frank knew it was time for another image. Pal Joey had become a liability. The sharp-suited shark whose voice and charm got him out of trouble was no image for a grown man who rubbed shoulders with the greatest powers in the world. Frank called his PR people in and got a goddamn mouthful about how it was his own fault for not sucking up to the press. Yeah, and where had that got him back in the early 50s? Nowheresville, buster, that was where. Nah, he needed to be seen to be doing some good. So, he put together a hot sextet of Bill Miller (piano), Al Viola (guitar), Ralph Pena (bass), Irv Cottler (drums), Emil Richards (vibes) and Harry Klee (sax and flute) and planned a world tour to raise $1 million for kids. Frank picked a set the band all knew, so he didn't have to rehearse with 'em, and kicked off in Mexico City on 15 April. It was a bit tough, but the guys would get it soon. Neal Hefti had written some good arrangements, Bill was a good band-leader. As they played Tokyo, Rome, Athens and Tel Aviv, things got better and better. By the time they hit Paris on 5 June, the band were swinging. Frank was skimming through some numbers, but there were a lot of songs, twenty six in all for Chrissakes. Generally, standards like Porter's I've Got You Under My Skin and I Get A Kick Out Of You had the band playing like they were a real jazz outfit. The quieter numbers were all Frank. Sammy and Jimmy's The Second Time Around, Rodgers and Hart's My Funny

Shirley MacLaine was the only dame to join the
Rat Pack – neither Frank nor Dino hit on her.

Valentine, and of course, Mercer and Arlen's One For My Baby, had minimal backing from the band. It was all these songs needed. By the time they reached an encore with Sammy and Jimmy's Come Fly With Me, Frank was looking forward to hearing this one back. He'd even keep that intro by Charles Aznavour on the record – what had the guy said? Whatever, it was real classy.

A week later Frank wandered into a small recording studio in London's Bayswater. He liked the place, it reminded him of the early Capitol sessions. Frank thought that recording an album there, of songs by British writers, was a good way of saying thank you to a country that had always been good to him. So, he'd had Mo Ostin book three days for him while he was over. A BBC guy, Robert Farnon had arranged and was conducting the songs – among them Ray Noble's The Very Thought Of You, Ivor Novello's We'll Gather Lilacs, Billy Reid's Gypsy and Noel Coward's I'll Follow My Secret Heart. Of course, Frank had also to record Sherwin and Maschwitz's A Nightingale Sang In Berkeley Square and Carroll Coates' London By Night.

A couple of weeks earlier, Frank's London shows had been totally over-subscribed (20,000 couldn't get in!), and rapturously received. Before the Paris show, the French Prez had given Frank some medal last handed out to JFK (he'd have to send a picture of that to Bobby). Frank was feeling better. His voice was getting a bit ragged, but the timing and phrasing was as perfect as he demanded. Plus, Hank had called to tell him that the Cal-Neva was almost finished. Time to go home.

COME BLOW YOUR HORN
Summer-Fall 1962

FRANK AND HANK were in the car, heading to Cal-Neva. Hank was bending the Leader's ear about Sam Giancana. Apparently Sam had been staying at the Lodge with Phyllis McGuire, and mouthing off about owning a chunk of the place. Hank was bellyaching about how if the Nevada Gaming Control Board found out, they'd all lose their licence, because Sam had not only been banned from casinos, but from the whole damn State.
Frank asked Hank what he wanted. He said he wanted out, but that the Lodge had eaten up all he had.
Frank, without the cash on him, gave the man ownership of his five publishing companies, and stopped the car. Hank got out, Frank drove off.
Later the next day, Frank got into a fight with a so-called deputy sheriff who was being disrespectful to an old

girlfriend of Frank's.

In terms of record sales, 1962 was a good year. As of mid-August, Sinatra albums had been on the charts nearly all year. Sinatra And Strings made number eight, whereas Point Of No Return only made nineteen but, as it was on Capitol, this didn't unduly bother Frank. The Capitol compilation Sings Of Love And Things made fifteen, Reprise's Swingin' Brass and All Alone made eighteen and twenty five respectively.

In September Frank started shooting a new movie, another kind of Pal Joey. Titled Come Blow Your Horn, it has Frank as a playboy who eventually learnt there was more to life than boozing and womanising.

In October Frank booked his dream date – two days with Count Basie and his orchestra, arranged by Neal Hefti. Frank was fond of saying how he'd dreamt of singing with the Count since he was seven years old. He wasn't joking.

They recorded it live, with the Count sitting, his damned sailor's hat pushed back, his back to Frank and bassist Buddy Catlett to the Count's left. Everyone else faced the two men, with Frank standing on a raised level singing, as usual, with his hands in his pockets.

The songs were great: Pennies From Heaven, The Tender Trap, Learnin' The Blues, I'm Gonna Sit Right Down And Write Myself A Letter and I Won't Dance were all familiar Sinatra songs, but the way the Count played 'em was new.

Of the new songs, Leslie Bricusse's My Kind Of Girl swung like no other. With the Count's rolling piano, New Orleans beat and extended middle eight full of syncopation, flute solo and walking bass, it was unlike any Sinatra number before, and sounded like a new Frank – the jazz singer.

GOODY GOODY
29 November-December 1962

'AND HERE HE IS, the star of our show, direct from the bar – Dean Martin.' Dino tripped onto the Villa Venice stage with cigarette and drink in hand. Matty Malneck kicked the Henry Brandon orchestra into Fisher, Goodwin and Shay's When You're Smiling. Dino sang a verse the writers hadn't come up with. 'When you're drinkin', when you're drinkin', the show looks good to you ... but when you're sober, the skies all seem grey. Yeah when you're sober, life's a pain. So keep drinkin' that's what I'm thinkin' 'cos that's what I love to do.' As the orchestra slipped seamlessly into Rodgers and Hart's The Lady Is A Tramp, Dino played the crowd, singing 'I love Chicago, it's carefree and gay, I'd even work here without any pay, I'll lay you odds it turns out that way, that's why this gentleman is a tramp'. The crowd loved it – they were hooting, clapping and laughing. Diamond-studded pinkie rings flashed, broads screamed, Martinis were downed. Standing at the back of the stage, Frank looked out at the biggest crowd of made guys he'd ever seen. This was a big favour Frank wanted to do for Sam Giancana. He, Dino and Sammy (as well as Eddie Fisher) were booked to perform a week at Sam's newly renovated club in the Chicago suburbs. The three played the gig as if it was The Sands. And it might well have been, since Giancana had a floating crap game out back for the high rollers pouring in to see the Clan from all around the country. Frank heard Sam was gonna make his dough ($3 million!) and pull back from things, lose the Feds, be a good boy. So, Dino warmed up the crowd – that stuff about his mother-in-law was great, 84 and don't need glasses, drinks straight out of the bottle – he was killin' 'em. And what class, thought Frank, doing Volare in Italian, and ending with On An Evening In Roma. Dino ran off as Frank came on and Matty struck up Goody Goody. Damn, they were slow! 'What are ya dragging back there, a tank?' Jeez, it was Matty's own goddamned song! OK, time for some shtick. The orchestra struck up a Dixie version of Sammy and Jimmy's Chicago. It limped a bit, but the sharkskin suits were tapping their Mary Janes. As Bill rolled the keys for When Your Lover Has Gone, Frank took a drink. It was Riddle's arrangement, they couldn't screw it up. A broad screamed and Frank ad-libbed, 'Where does it hurt, baby?'

But still he sounded like his heart was breaking. It was time for Frank to talk to his audience. He took his shoes off and reminisced about the Toddlin' Town – the Pump Room, old friends and whisky. Then he laid into Dino – 'the drunk who was just out here', Sammy – 'Smokey the bear', and Matty – 'Stay outta the sun, willya, you're peelin'. Then he really laid into gossip columnist Dorothy Killgallen – 'I met a lotta male finks, but I never met a female fink until I met Dorothy Killgallen! I wouldn't mind if she was a good-looking fink. The town she came from, they had a beauty contest when she was 17, and nobody won.' Man, did he give her a going over. That felt good. Time for a song he'd just recorded with Count Basie, Please Be Kind. Frank introduced it as being a recording for his new company, Reprise – the crowd clapped and chinked their glasses – Frank said 'thanks, partners'. Matty did his best, Hefti's score was good, but the Basie band they weren't. To round off his twenty-minute set, Frank introduced 'a saloon song' and jived Matty some about his lisp. Frank mock-scatted the opening bars, You're Nobody 'Til Somebody Loves You. 'Sing it Frank!' screamed a broad. 'No, I'm playing polo up here,' he replied. It was a high-kicking finale, Frank clung to the high notes, his right arm floating to the side as he dragged them out. The crowd were on their feet before the band had stopped. Frank left the stage and Sammy ran on. 'Good evening ladies and gentlemen, my name is Harry Belafonte.' As he completed the opening line of What Kind Of Fool Am I, Frank butted in, 'You're a schmuck'. Sammy barely managed ten minutes before, as he hit Hey There, Frank and Dino invaded the stage. For the next hour all three men laughed, joked and sang. It was the most fun three guys could have had without getting fruity. They didn't have to be paid to do this stuff. Which was just as well, since they weren't.

THE CONCERT SINATRA

18-21 February 1963

THE CONCERT SINATRA
ARRANGED AND CONDUCTED BY NELSON RIDDLE
HAVE DREAMED ■ MY HEART STOOD STILL ■ LOST IN THE STARS ■ OL' MAN RIVER
YOU'LL NEVER WALK ALONE ■ BEWITCHED ■ THIS NEARLY WAS MINE ■ SOLILOQUY
FROM CAROUSEL

This album utilizes Westrex 35MM recording, 24 RCA
44BX microphones, 8 track 21 position mixer console,
73 musicians, and 4 Sound Stages of the Goldwyn Studios in Hollywood. It represents an unparalleled achievement in the technology of Sound.

reprise

K 44001
STEREO

IT MADE FRANK happy to see his album with Basie make the highest chart position he'd had since I Remember Tommy. The week before going into Goldwyn's new, state-of-the-art studio with Nelson Riddle, Frank had given his parents a big New Jersey party for their fiftieth wedding anniversary. He was in a good mood. They had eleven songs to do, among them Rodgers and Hammerstein's Soliloquy. It was the reason Frank had wanted to do the film Carousel (he'd pulled out because they wanted him to do every take at least twice, and the bums weren't gonna pay him twice). At over eight minutes long, the song was some challenge. Sure he'd done it twice with Axel in the space of a month, back in the 40s, but Frank didn't feel those were great recordings. He'd try it late in the sessions.

Man! Those strings sounded good, and he could really hear himself clearly. This was the best Ol' Man River he'd ever done. Frank had been including the Kern and Hammerstein tune in all those shows last year, and he knew it pretty well. He was close to the mic, but not popping, he could lean into those bent notes. It sounded epic, tragic. Hairs were standing up on his neck.

The next day, Frank tried to give the same treatment to another Rodgers and Hammerstein song he'd also recorded in the 40s with Axel. You'll Never Walk Alone had the potential of being a Sinatra signature tune, he knew it. But somehow, it just didn't feel right. Sure, he was grabbing the notes and holding them, but it didn't feel edgy like Ol' Man River. The same day, Frank eased through Rodgers and Hammerstein's This Nearly Was Mine before finishing with one of their songs from The

King And I, the soft, sublimely romantic I Have Dreamed.

On the following day, Frank really relaxed into the new, lush treatment of Bewitched. He wasn't so sure about Sammy and Jimmy's California with its thick vocal chorus. The song, like Bass and Ward's America The Beautiful, seemed a bit over the top. A love song to a State, for Chrissakes? It looked good on paper, and Nelson's arrangements were great. It just seemed a bit forced, to Frank. It wasn't the best preparation for the last day's recording, and Soliloquy. The next evening, Frank wanted to go straight to it. The recording took some time, with its time changes, shifting tones and lines that scanned strangely. The studio lights had been turned off because they hummed too much. Frank stood, his hands in his pockets as usual, his hat tilted back and the side of his face illuminated by the light from his music stand. Frank acted the song as only he knew how. No rehearsal, just pulling on the feelings he'd had when Nancy told him she was pregnant for the first time all those years ago. He'd thought it would be a boy then, and of course it wasn't. At the end, Frank knew he had something special. He was happy, but the voice was a little shot. The final number of the session, You Brought A New Kind Of Love To Me wasn't the best he'd done it. Still, this had been a very good session. Frank had concentrated and worked hard. These songs were classic American numbers that nice folk would like. Frank didn't want everyone thinking he was just a hood. He wanted an album which even that tightass Bobby Kennedy could play for his children.

SINATRA'S SINATRA
29, 30 April 1963

CAPITOL HAD CONTINUED to re-work Frank's back catalogue. Something he would have loved to do himself, but Reprise didn't have enough stuff to make a package. So, he thought, why not do the good stuff again? What were the best songs he had recorded up to that point? He'd ask people – Frank Jr, Nancy maybe. Ten songs were chosen, and re-recorded over two days. They weren't the definitive versions, Frank knew that. But Under My Skin swung good and hard and Nancy (he changed a line or two) was nice. All The Way he kinda liked, and Witchcraft was kooky. At the end of the sessions, Mo Ostin said there should be a dozen songs, so Frank recalled Sammy and Jimmy's Call Me Irresponsible from the Come Blow Your Horn title session recorded on 21 January. Nelson said he liked Sammy and Jimmy's Pocketful Of Miracles – which Frank had recorded in November 1961 for Sinatra And Strings, but which hadn't been used because Don Costa had arranged everything else – so this too was added.

SHOWTUNES
July, August 1963

THE PREZ WASN'T returning Frank's calls. Sam was still visiting the Cal-Neva, which wasn't doing the business it ought to. Jilly Rizzo, the New York bar owner who'd taken Hank's place at Frank's side, said Sam was shooting his mouth off again about owning a piece of the Lodge. The music business had changed unrecognisably. Presley wasn't King of the charts anymore, but there were all these new bands with guitars and long hair who wrote their own childish, three-minute songs. Nancy kept bugging him and Mo to let her record a rock song. Maybe they ought to let her, it wasn't as if a whole load of other Reprise records were selling. Christ, Sam's pal Johnny Rosselli could get any disc on any jukebox in the country,

and Frank himself hadn't had a hit single since 1960. Mo just shrugged and said the kids wanted guitars, love and sex. Frank should be looking to appeal to their parents – the nice people. Frank hit on an idea to record a whole bunch of Broadway shows and put 'em in a four-album box set. He'd got Dino, Sammy, Crosby, Debbie Reynolds, the McGuires, Keely Smith, even Rosemary Clooney to record Finian's Rainbow (hey, he had a bunch of that stuff recorded already), Guys And Dolls (that would show Brando how to sing), Kiss Me Kate and South Pacific (well, that goddamned movie soundtrack was the biggest selling record ever). He was going to show them how Broadway shows should sound. It would be the first time Frank Sinatra appeared on a disc as Producer.

In the middle of the sessions for Musical Repertory Theatre, Frank got together with Marty Paich to record Wells and Segal's Here's To The Losers. It was a saloon tune which Frank liked, that was upbeat – almost mocking. Frank sang it like Sammy Davis would have done. He would put it on an album later. Frank, Dino and Sammy recorded We Open In Venice at the same session on 10 July that Frank and Dino recorded Guys And Dolls (although that version wouldn't be used – too much fun). At the end of July, Frank, Dino and Crosby recorded Frank Loesser's Fugue For Tinhorns and The Oldest Established (Permanent Floating Crap Game In New York). After a summer singing goody-goody tunes for square hicks, Frank and the Clan needed some Vegas time.

The
Summit at
home.
During
daylight!

THE SUMMIT
September 1963

FRANK AND THE CLAN moved to The Sands for a two-week residency. Frank was determined to release a live recording. Everyone had been telling him how, when they all got together, they were unbeatable – a rib-cracker act. Even Frank's hulk of a bodyguard, Frankie Shaw, would double up with laughter while they were on stage. And Frankie wouldn't laugh at nothing. Reprise taped six shows straight, in which Frank sang Hefti, Riddle and May arrangements of recently recorded songs. Unfortunately, the orchestra wasn't really up to Frank's exacting standards. He couldn't release the stuff. But he sure enjoyed fooling around with Dino and Sammy.

Man, Frank needed it. The Nevada Gaming Board had given him a hard time about playing golf with Sam Giancana at Cal-Neva. He'd told them that he didn't invite Sam to Nevada, he just ran in to him coming out of his girlfriend Phyllis' cabin. What should he have done, pretend he didn't see him? Then the bums had sent a couple of investigating officers down while the tables were cashing up, so Frank had them sent them away. He didn't know, but Skinny had offered the pair of them $100 each to leave. Now they were claiming attempted intimidation, that Frank had been lying to the board and violating gaming laws by having Giancana over to the lodge. At the end of the month, the Nevada Gaming Board Of Control tried to revoke Frank's licence, whilst letting the whole world know he would be under investigation. This all just hit Frank as he was negotiating to lose the headache of running Reprise, by selling two-thirds of it to Warners. Frank, though, would remain a director.

Mickey Rudin, Frank's lawyer heard from Jack Warner that they couldn't have someone as director who was involved in a big fight with Gaming Control over mobsters. Frank couldn't fight the Control Board. Fuck it, the place was losing money anyway.

And man, what a laugh Bobby Kennedy would have if Frank was investigated. Frank turned in his gaming licence, and dumped Cal-Neva. While all of this was going down, Frank Jr made his debut as a singer, and with the Tommy Dorsey band at that. He got fair reviews, even from his old man.

STAY WITH ME
October-December 1963

ON 13 OCTOBER Frank laid the vocal track of Martin and Blane's Have Yourself A Merry Little Christmas over orchestral tracks laid down back in April. It'd be nice to have a Christmas hit. Frank was feeling mellow. He'd pulled off the coup of getting Crosby, Edward G Robinson and Peter Falk (a funny little guy) to commit to a new movie, Robin And The Seven Hoods – with Frank, Dino and Sammy as the do-good Hoods. Lawford he'd written out of the deal. They were making it in Chicago. What a kick in the head to Bobby Kennedy! Frank would show him what a sense of humour was.

When news of the assassination of JFK reached Frank, he was filming in a cemetery, near a headstone bearing the name Kennedy. A light went off in his head, but he had to finish the film. Unfortunately, the finished article looks just as if Frank has heard someone close to him died. All the jokes fall flat – the Mafia jokes seem morbid and ominous, rather than belly-laughs. For three days after filming finished, Frank buried himself in the bedroom at his Palm Springs house, surrounded by the things the Prez had used while at Frank's place. Who did it? Why? Frank ran all the possibilities through his mind. It couldn't have been Sam's people, he'd have heard. Frank's pal Sidney Korshak, the mainman lawyer for the Families would have told him. Wouldn't he?

Frank cancelled a proposed benefit show for Martin Luther King Jr on 26 November. But he kept to the recording date he'd set for 3 December. Don Costa was a good guy. He just let Frank do the songs – Dolan and Mercer's Talk To Me Baby, and Moross and Leigh's Stay With Me (Theme from The Cardinel) – and get out. Frank was distracted, his spirits were low. He'd said he wanted The Manchurian

Candidate withdrawn. It was too close for comfort.

Five days later, on 8 December, Frank Jr, who was only 19, was kidnapped before making an appearance with the Dorsey band in Lake Tahoe. Within hours of the kidnapping, Frank was in Reno. Bobby Kennedy was being a stand-up guy about it, and had the whole of the FBI on the case. Agents were guarding Nancy, Nancy Jr and even his parents. Three days later Frank was given the run around by the kidnappers and sent to Carson City. They wanted $240,000 in used bills, and told Frank, who was on a payphone in a gas station, to go back to LA and they'd finalise things there. The day before Frank's forty-eighth birthday, a drop was made, and Frank drove alone to the pick-up point to get his son. He wasn't there. Frank went home to Nancy and, four hours later, Frank Jr turned up in a G-Man's car trunk. He was alive and well. Frank was shattered. What a fucking year. Jackie O sent him a note after Christmas, thanking Frank for being 'so thoughtful', and commenting on how the only happy thing to have happened this year was the safe return of Frank Jr. The dame got it about right. The next year could only be better.

AMERICA I HEAR YOU SINGING
January-April 1964

NOW, MORE THAN ever, America needed to believe in itself. With Frank Jr recovering in Palm Springs, Frank recorded a bunch of patriotic songs with old-time troupers Fred Waring and his Pennsylvanians at the usual place, Studio One off Sunset. Riddle arranged Burke and Van Heusen's Early American and Allen and Robinson's The House I Live In (and did a better job than Axel had managed almost twenty years earlier), Jack Halloran arranged Raye, Prince and Black's You're A Lucky Fellow, Mr Smith. Crosby also contributed to the project, recording Let Us Break Bread Together and a Sammy and Jimmy tune, You

Never Had It So Good. Crosby was persuaded to join Reprise – which Frank had finally sold to Warners. Mo kept his job. So the Chairman had to make a new album.

Sticking vaguely with an American theme, Frank and Nelson decided to do an album of Academy Award winning songs – including, of course his own Three Coins In A Fountain. He added Burke and Van Heusen's Swinging On A Star for the first time, a somewhat duller The Continental, a softly swinging The Way You Look Tonight, with its haunting sense of longing, and a fair Secret Love.

Almost immediately after completing the recording, Frank started shooting his first film as director, None But The Brave. In Tokyo, of all places. Frank liked the World War II storyline of American and Japanese soldiers becoming pals, but then having to kill each other for a greater truth.

In early April, Frank, Dino, Sammy and Crosby had to go back into the studio to record songs for Robin And The Seven Hoods, with Frank performing his definitive My Kind Of Town. By this time, the bums who'd kidnapped Frank Jr had been arrested and claimed they were put up to the job as part of a publicity stunt. Goddamned expensive stunt. As Frank said, 'This family needs publicity like it needs peritonitis.' The jury convicted them.

The Leader (at back, behind the Count) in the studio with the Basie band. A dream come true for Frank.

IT MIGHT AS WELL BE SWING
May-December 1964

'THAT'LL TEACH ME to be a hero,' thought Frank as he lay, gasping for breath on the beach at Lihue on the Pacific island of Kauai. He'd tried to swim out to producer Howard Koch's wife, Ruth who was in some trouble. But as a wave crashed down on him, she passed him heading for shore and he was swept out to sea. For half an hour he tried to swim back in. Jilly was running around trying to find a boat, some guy jumped in the sea with his surfboard and a couple of other guys swam out, too. They had to drag Frank back. God damn, what a way to make a movie. These people need a rescue boat. Frank bought them one.

Before heading back to LA, Frank decided to hire a new arranger for his planned album with the Basie band. Plenty of people had recommended this cat, Quincy Jones, to Frank, and he'd liked the stuff Basie had suggested he hear. Frank gave the kid a bunch of tunes to arrange, and had him stay in Dino's dressing room next to Frank's cottage in Hawaii while they finished None But The Brave. Q, as Frank called him, was quickly initiated into Rat Pack ways. Frank would wind down after a day's shoot with Q and Bill. They'd slug some JD, pick out the numbers and swing some. And man, they swung. Frank had been playing Fly Me To The Moon in his Vegas set for some time, but he hadn't recorded it yet. Q took it out of the waltz time it had been written in, and adapted Frank's Bossa Nova beat to make it swing-time. The result was the definitive version – the one which Frank would always use. Wilson and Trenet's I Wish You Love built up through summery verses with Frank's seductive voice talking the lyrics, to a full-flowering, spectacular end.

Frank Loesser's I Believe In You began with a hurried, rim-shot-driven, brass-inflected verse, building excitedly to a funny little downbeat end. Ortolani, Olivero, Ciorciolina and Newell's More kept the beat running, its underlying 4/4 beat driving sweeping strings with Frank's laid-back vocal suggesting a louche lover, rather than the lost soul proclaiming love that the lyrics supposed. Don Gibson's I Can't Stop Loving You was given the same blues-piano treatment as Ray Charles's hit version of two years earlier, with Frank sounding weary and accepting of his dilemma, rather than cut up about it. Jerry Herman's Hello Dolly was pure big band hokum, but man, those soundtracks were selling like hot-cakes. Rather than the schmaltz of Satchmo's version though, Basie's band kicked up a storm with Harry Sweets Edison treating Satchmo's trumpet part with economy, and Frank dedicating a verse to Louis, singing 'Hello Satch ... promise you won't go away again.' The Count even allowed himself a brief solo before Frank bowed out with a Satchmo 'Oh Yeah!' Mercy and Vemmerstett's I Wanna Be Around allowed the band and Frank a little breather from the roaring pace. Frank positively revelled in the lyrics, particularly the line 'And that's when I'll discover that revenge is sweet', broadcasting it with power and holding onto the notes clearly and strongly. Q's treatment of Coleman and Leigh's The Best Is Yet To Come was to become, like Fly Me To The Moon, the definitive version for Frank (and an army of impersonators). A song of impending promise and high hopes, Frank started it with an understated, flip delivery, revealing a confident man who refused to get over-excited. But the horns showed no restraint, as they soared, swooped, pushed and implored, while the rhythm section held as steady as the Count's sparse piano. The song played out quietly, with the almost menacing promise 'come the day you're mine' hanging over the simmering, dying horns. Sacha Distel and Jack Reardon's The Good Life had the gentle swing of the French singer's slow finger-snap, but as usual Frank made it sound like no-one could ever do it this way, this good (Q mentioned to Frank that Sammy Davis could impersonate everyone except him). As if to show that Frank understood that the world was changing, the record was closed by Bacharach and David's Wives And Lovers. David's lyrics implored young women to remember that wives have to be lovers too. In truth it was not the strongest song Bacharach and David had written, and it was the weak point of what Frank knew was the strongest album he'd made since, well, the last one he'd made with the Count. But it was still a fine recording.

The next week Frank and Crosby went back into the studio with Fred Waring to record a Christmas album. Great timing! Almost 100 degrees outside, and they were singing about An Old-Fashioned Christmas. Jeez, what a racket. Still, it kept Frank in training for a new album of ballads.

Softly As I Leave You was part arranged by Ernie Freeman, and part by Nelson Riddle. There were also two Billy May arrangements, only one of which made it onto the record, Coleman and Leigh's Pass Me By. Frank didn't bother keeping Glazer and Solomon's Since Marie Left Me. The album felt even to Frank like a gap-filler. It had some middle-of-the-road singalong bullshit stuff, like Baker Knight's Anytime At All alongside the ballads and swing numbers. It wasn't a whole record. Frank knew that he had to get back to emotional ballads. It would take some time, and he'd have to get Gordon Jenkins to arrange, but he would for the next weepy.

By October the Academy Awards album (Days Of Wine & Roses, Moon River and other Academy Award Winners) had made ten on the charts, while America I Hear You Singing had only made 116. Smoothy Andy Williams had hit huge with Days Of Wine & Roses – what was going on? It Might As Well Be Swing failed to make the Top Ten, stalling at thirteen. By the year's end Softly As I Leave You would just scrape into the top twenty, at nineteen. The year's charts had been dominated by a new band, and a new sound. The Beatles had invaded America. Frank hadn't dismissed the four moptop English bums like he had Presley almost ten years before. He knew something was happening. The death of the Prez had opened his eyes to what was going down in the world at large, not just in Vegas, Chicago, New York and LA. The world was changing. Would he? Could he?

Frank had met a new woman – a child, almost – who turned him on. Though younger than Nancy, she had an old soul. Mia Farrow, an actress Frank had met on the set of his stupid new movie, Von Ryan's Express (cowboys and indians in uniform, Frank had said), was to change his life for him.

Frank and Dino playing themselves. At one point Dino forgot to duck a punch. and landed on his back. From where he bit Sinatra's ankle.

"FOUR FOR TEXAS"

ALDRICH CO.		470-22
SCENE 284dn 320		LOCATION Stage 3
SET STILL		ExT. WARHOUSE DOOR
		And
DATE 7-9-63		INT. WARHOUSE

SEPTEMBER OF MY YEARS
January-July 1965

NONE BUT THE Brave opened to good reviews in the first month of the year. It did well at the box office too. In February Frank and old-pal Joe E Lewis headlined two weeks in Miami before heading for The Sands. It was good to see the wiseguys. In March Frank started a new, dumbass comedy (Marriage On The Rocks) with Dino and Debbie Kerr in which he played a dull executive whose wife wanted a divorce. They went to Mexico, blah blah blah. Nancy got to play his daughter for fun instead of for real. During filming Nancy's husband Tommy Sands did a bunk. As far as Frank was concerned, she was better off without the jerk. Frank finally got around to recording with Jenkins in April, but not until he had sent a blank cheque to old friend George Raft, who was being investigated by the IRS.

In December Frank was 50. It was a time to reflect. September Of My Years was to be a blues album with strings, like Sinatra And Strings had been, but this time the songs were not to be about anyone but the singer. Jimmy and Sammy were writing the title number, as usual. So the sessions started with Sunny Skylar's Don't Wait Too Long, a warning to Mia perhaps, not to resist temptation, beginning as it did with the line 'You are the summer, I am the autumn, don't wait too long'. The reeds twittered like birds, the strings plucked like falling leaves and ironically, Frank sounded like he did some twenty years before. For the third and final time, Frank recorded Weill and Anderson's September Song (the album's endpiece), and for the first time, sounded like he meant it. It was the second time that Frank had recorded Arlen and Yip Harburg's Last Night When We Were Young. The arrangement was not as bright as Riddle's, but Frank's voice now had the age and edge to make it work. The same was true for Rodgers and Hammerstein's Hello Young Lovers, which had first been arranged by Axel in 51. The new songs worked best, however. Sammy and Jimmy's It Gets Lonely Early matched Frank like his suit. A glorious Loser song, it had a reflective air, haunting strings, a lone bell and Frank sounding as if he meant every word. Gordon Jenkins's own This Is All I Ask, set the tone: 'As I approach the prime of my life, I

find I have the time of my life, learning to enjoy at my leisure, all simple pleasures'. Of course it was a deceit, but as with all Sinatra deceits, it was a good one, just like Jenkins's How Old Am I?, in which Frank let everyone know he was now as grown up as he should be ('Don't mind these lines underneath my eyes'). Frank liked his deceits – they were almost truths, some of what these songs said about him were true.

Songs such as Bart Howard's The Man In The Looking Glass, for example. A first-person narrative, this dealt with the physical proof of growing old in a less sophisticated, funny, but just as effective way as Ervin Drake's It Was A Very Good Year (which had first been recorded by the Kingston Trio four years earlier). Where Looking Glass was slightly comic – Frank asked his reflection 'How is your sacro-iliac?' – by contrast, Good Year was tragic. From its harp and clarinet intro, through the recounting of the years from 17 to 21 and 35 to 50, the song was unashamedly heart-wrenching and melancholic. As with all the great Sinatra songs, Frank understood the value of a good, emotive yarn. It Was A Very Good Year – just like In The Wee Small Hours, All Or Nothing At All and My Kind Of Town before it – was a defining Sinatra tune. Frank knew people would see it as autobiographical. Hell, he almost believed it himself.

There was almost a month between sessions before Frank could record the title song. It was worth the wait. The song was suitably 'autobiographical', with Frank singing about himself with a mixture of regret and pride. In it he admitted being wayward but how now, in his autumn years, he could look back longingly to the great love of his life and missed opportunities. It was a classic Cahn, Van Heusen song which tugged at the listener's emotions, in much the same way as the strings that adorned the tune.

Back on top of the charts, and back on television.

EVERYBODY HAS THE RIGHT TO BE WRONG (AT LEAST ONCE)
Summer-December 1965

WITH ALL THAT Autumn of his life stuff done, Frank wanted to enjoy that Summer. He had a semi-compilation album planned, My Kind Of Broadway for which, on 23 August, he recorded Sammy and Jimmy's Everybody Has The Right To Be Wrong (At Least Once). It was a smack in the mouth to all those who were bad-mouthing Frank for taking Mia on a cruise with him off the New England coast. There had been more press around the Southern Breeze than there were fish. So he'd said he would never re-marry, but hey, everybody had the right to change their mind – not least Frank Sinatra.

Frank also recorded Jimmy and Sammy's I'll Only Miss Her When I Think Of Her (like Everybody Has, from Skyscraper) plus Jacobson and Roberts's Golden Moment (from Hot September) at that session. The rest of the album was composed of previously recorded showtunes, such as Have You Met Miss Jones, Hello Dolly (from the Basie sessions) and Luck Be A Lady Tonight (arranged by Billy May).

In July Frank had played a short tour, closing the Newport Jazz Festival with Count Basie, before doing three nights with the Count in Long Island and then two nights in Chicago. In September Dino called Frank 'Chairman of the Board' in public for the first time on his TV show.

In October Frank re-recorded a number of songs to be included on a double-album retrospective which would accompany a television special. Frank figured he wasn't going to write an autobiography, so why not make a musical one? Frank narrated A Man & His Music, and chose the thirty one songs. He also included September 1963's live recording at The Sands. What did anyone expect? It was the prime-time, squeaky-clean Sinatra story. There was some truly great music, even though none of it was new. A Man & His Music would make number nine by Christmas, following up on the success of September Of My Years which made five. Compilation Sinatra 65 made nine, but My Kind Of Broadway only managed thirty. Someone at Reprise suggested Frank should do another theme album, like Come Fly With Me.

In November Frank went into the studio with Nelson Riddle to record Moonlight Sinatra. The idea was that all the songs would be about the moon. Frank wasn't sure about the idea, but most of the songs were good. Miller and Parish's Moonlight Serenade, with Frank's voice swamped in reverb, somehow managed to lose the Glenn Miller stigma, making it sound like a different song completely. Riddle smartly used no banks of horns. Burke and Van Heusen's Oh You Crazy Moon sounded like one of the dirtiest, sleaziest burlesque, nightclub-damnation-of-love numbers Frank had managed. But on the whole, the moon was yellow. When it was released early in 1966, Moonlight Sinatra would only manage number thirty four on the charts.

Mia Farrow was almost half Frank's age when they met. Dino cabled Frank, 'I've got Scotch older than her' when they married.

AT THE SANDS
January-April 1966

FRANK HAD REACHED fifty and had still not released a live album he was really proud of. He had 26 January to 1 February booked with the Basie band at The Sands, and had a couple of days free before recording started. So he flew the Count and his boys out to rehearse. This was going to be the one. Ten different shows were recorded, the orchestra conducted by Quincy Jones (who Frank praised highly during performances). It was the great live album Frank wanted. As well as the songs, which included a jumping Come Fly With Me, a kicking I've Got You Under My Skin, a heart-wrenching It Was A Very Good Year and a truly sad Don't You Worry About Me, there was a lot of Sinatra patter. He told his life story in brief, ribbed his father over his speech, made a dig at Dino for using his own jokes (the one about buying his ma-in-law a house which the police kept closing down), joked about Sammy Davis and even himself. The Basie band swung, Frank had fun, it was a great live album.

STRANGERS IN THE NIGHT
April-October 1966

IT WAS ALWAYS fun sitting in on Dino's recording sessions. Frank would chat up the broads, tell the orchestra where they were going wrong, joke with Dag and generally fool around. By the end of the session on 11 April at which Dino recorded Today Is Not The Day, Frank was dying to get started. Apparently someone had heard that Jack Jones and Bobby Darin wanted to do this new song – a Bert Kaempfert tune for which Charlie Singleton and Eddie Snyder had added lyrics. Strangers In The Night, arranged by Ernie Freeman, sounded to Frank like another defining moment. It was odd – not a typical Sinatra song. Almost a blues number, the swirling strings are underpinned by a very hip tambourine and snare, the song breaking into a quick bossa nova, almost stopping completely before a kitsch build-up to a grandstand finale. Frank found himself humming Dooby dooby doo because he'd ended before the band. Did he want to do it again? Nah, the humming was good, unusual. The words spoke of an illicit affair, which to Frank sounded very 'now', as his daughter Nancy was always saying. Frank liked it enough to suggest releasing it as a single.

On 7 May Strangers In The Night entered the Billboard singles chart, and climbed to number one. It was Frank's first top-slot single in twenty years. On 11 May Frank took Nelson Riddle into the studio to make an album to go around Strangers. Instead of brass, Riddle pushed a Hammond organ to the front of the arrangements, using its effects to colour tunes in the way different reeds had done ten years earlier.

Picking new tunes like Tony Hatch's Call Me and Downtown, and slotting them alongside new-to-Frank numbers such as Mayer and Mercer's Summer Wind, Rodgers and Hart's The Most Beautiful Girl In The World, and Lerner and Lane's On A Clear Day (You Can See Forever), gave the album a cool appeal. The Beatles, Beach Boys, Bob Dylan and company were all paying respect to Frank, saying nice things about him, praising his style. The time was right for Frank to speak to a new generation. The fact that he'd stood up for accused Communists during McCarthyism lent him a radical air. His joke on At The Sands about Dino being stoned more times than American Embassies got great laughs, and showed he was hip to what was happening. Most of all the Hammond Organ, which was being so over-used on all the psychedelic rock albums, made Frank's record hip.

An air of cool breezed through the record – from Frank's skewed, understated treatment of My Baby Just Cares For Me, on which he sounded so relaxed he could be stoned (and not just on JD), to his slurred delivery of Downtown, with its Stax-influenced parping horns, chopping rhythm and almost oriental strings. Added to this his near-parodying performance of Yes Sir, That's My Baby and it was hard to believe that it was the product of someone over thirty, let alone fifty. Sinatra was undeniably hip, and happening.

Once again Frank ruled the roost. At Dino's forty-ninth birthday party, Frank got into a scuffle with some wiseass who thought he was a tough guy. Frank was almost untouched – the guy got a fractured skull. In July Frank played the Sands. Mia was waiting in the wings and on the 14th they announced their engagement. Five days later, at Sands manager Jack Entratter's house, they were married. Even Nancy Jr wasn't invited. Bitch Ava said, 'I always knew he'd end up in bed with a little boy.' It seemed that hell hath no fury …? The next week Frank was too happy to sing and ditched a session with Ernie Freeman for new album, That's Life. In August, Frank campaigned for Democrat Pat Brown as governor of California, standing against Ronald Reagan, who had testified for the Feds against so-called Commies back in the early 50s. He also heard that fink Reagan was a Fed informer. Unfortunately the bum won. Frank and Mia bought a house in Bel Air, and did it up while they stayed in Palm Springs. Life was good, things were going well.

THAT'S LIFE
November-December 1966

WHEN FRANK was with Mia, he was sweetness itself. She made him feel like an innocent again and she kept him away from the Board. When they got married, Dino had sent Frank a message that he'd got a Scotch older than Mia. Every day was Summer with Mia, they had the sun, the sea, a ton of pressmen and each other. Back at The Sands though, Frank was again the Chairman. It was a different world, where people wore black and business was done. Frank had to be the man the people paid to see. 'So you probably heard I got married,' he told his first night audience. 'Yeah, I know I wasn't gonna do it again, but I finally found a broad I could cheat on.' Big laughs – big, big laughs from the pearls and cufflinks out front. Big tears from Mia. She wasn't Ava.

A month before opening at his casino, Frank had recorded Kay and Gordon's That's Life as a follow-up single to Strangers. To Frank, the song sounded like it was in the same groove musically, and he loved the lyrical sentiment.

Yeah, he'd been a puppet, a pauper, a pirate, a poet, a pawn, a king – he'd always picked himself up and gotten back on top. It was a great cry of determination, of hope and cynicism. Frank's throat was ragged. His performance was one of the rawest he'd committed to tape.

Frank doing the Academy Awards his way.

But he liked it that way. The Hammond organ was less conspicuous than on Strangers, but then Ernie Freeman didn't want it to sound like anyone else, did he? Ernie put a big vocal chorus behind Frank instead, the way soundtracks and TV shows were using them. He had structured the backing like Stax or Motown were doing, with big snares, and beat-driven horns. Freeman used the same chorus for Harbert's Give Her Love and Becaud and Sigman's What Now My Love for the album, which Frank recorded after The Sands. What Now My Love was one of Frank's favourite numbers with its finger-clicking swing-beat, swaying background chorus and world-weary lyrics. The soaring strings and brass gave the song a kind of up, a jetset swing which was becoming all the rage. Again, Frank's voice was a little ragged around the edges – his Vegas throat had not completely cleared up. Still, he made all the notes and held on to them, even on Limey Geoff Stevens's wacky Winchester Cathedral. The song was an oddball – Ernie did his best with it, but it wasn't completely satisfactory. Frank wasn't sure if turning it into a burlesque number was weird enough to appeal to the kids. Webster and Jarre's Somewhere My Love (from Dr Zhivago) was more familiar territory, if difficult to get excited about. Sand And Sea, Gilbert Becaud, Mike Vidalin and Mack David's snazzy, laid-back surf number was fun, though. Frank almost drawled his way through the number. He could see Malibu as he closed his eyes and tilted his head back, adopting his usual hands-in-pockets stance. LeGrand and Gimbel's I Will Wait For You was almost the opposite – its melodramatic string crescendo opening leading into Frank's solo, before settling into a marching declaration of undimming love. Frank felt the vocal chorus was again used to colour the background and that this ultimately failed to lift the number. The sessions ended with Andre and Dory Previn's You're Gonna Hear From Me, a little song which Frank did his best to make epic. It was not quite the defiant shout of individualism Frank was looking for, but it was a fitting finale to an album of half-chances. That's Life was a hit, making the Top-Five singles chart again, which was good, coming after Summer Wind's failure to make the Top Twenty. Frank knew he had to do something different to keep that buzz of success ringing in his head.

For the first sing-through of Something Stupid, Frank sang like Daffy Duck.

SOMETHIN' STUPID
January-July 1967

THE NEW YEAR had started with a party. Frank was celebrating a year in which in Strangers In The Night he'd had his first number one album for six years. He had then seen the subsequent two releases make the Top Ten, At The Sands peaking at nine, and That's Life making six. So Frank, in Miami at the Eden Roc with old pals Jilly, Sam and co, held a 65th birthday bash for Joe E Lewis. Hell, why not? Frank had been subpoenaed by the Feds to appear before a Grand Jury later in the month. They wanted to talk to him about Mob money in Vegas. Big fuckin' deal. Sidney Korshak had given Frank a few pointers, and behind closed doors, he'd told them enough to make sure they didn't take it any further.

At the end of the month, Frank went into the studio with a whole new set-up. He'd loved what he'd heard of Brazilian guitarist Antonio Carlos Jobim's music, and knew that the laid-back, gentle South American rhythms would ease his aching throat. Using a new arranger, Claus Ogerman and some subtle string players, Frank duetted with Jobim on his second recording of Baubles, Bangles And Beads, his third version of I Concentrate On You, as well as first attempts at Jobim's own Girl From Ipanema and How Insensitive. Frank sang Jobim's haunting Dindi alone, and delivered the only version of the song truly worth hearing. Using Al Viola on guitar for Berlin's Change Partners, and keeping the same smooth, string-swathed backing for the rest of the four tracks which made up the album, Frank delivered a complete, themed record of cool sounds. Francis Albert Sinatra & Antonio Carlos Jobim demonstrated in a way that no other release since And Strings in 1962 had, that Frank still had the power to turn an album into a work of seductive art.

At the end of the third day of recording, Frank laid down another definitive saloon song, Johnny Mercer and Doris Tauber's Drinking Again, pouring the ache into it like the water in his beloved JD. To round off the sessions, Frank finally gave in to Nancy Jr's pleading, and let her in the studio with her arranger, Billy Strange. C Carson Parks's Somethin' Stupid sounded like a dumb song to Frank, but his little girl wanted to do it so ... During the first run-through Frank sounded all his S's like Daffy Duck would've done it. That relaxed Nancy, and they got it on the second time round. Nancy sang the melody straight, keeping strictly to the notes, while her father performed vocal miracles. In the final mix the strings, trumpets and Spanish guitar filled out Nancy's middle-ground, while Frank floated above, below and around the melody, leading the song through its gentle path. In the end, even Frank had to admit it was two and a half minutes of pure pop pleasure.

Mo Ostin bet Frank two bucks the single would bomb. By the end of April it would top the charts around the world, and sell over a million copies. Ostin didn't pay up.

In June and July Frank returned to the studio to record songs for an album to go around Somethin' Stupid. For a change, he had different guys arrange and conduct the songs. Ernie Freeman took the baton for a Kaempfert, Rehbein and Sigman number, The World We Knew, and added his trademark chorus. It over-pumped a dull song. He did the same to Tony Hatch and Jackie Trent's Don't Sleep In The Subway and, in the process, almost turned it into a novelty record. The chorus was too upfront, the horns too gimmicky. No wonder Frank sounded out of sorts, he was almost swamped by the mess piling on top of him. Hell, all he could do was think like Sammy Davis Jr, and try to scat his way out of it. At least Ernie treated Charlie Chaplin's This Is My Song in a straightforward manner, all strings and Waltz time. Gordon Jenkins was his usual reliable self, turning both Jim Harbert's This Is My Love and Sukman and Webster's You Are There into warm, comfortable, string-swathed songs of quiet beauty. However even he couldn't save Don Black and Dave Barry's Born Free, a saccharine-sweet slice of cheesecake. Both Jenkins and Frank tried their hardest, but the best they could manage was to keep it understated. Billy Strange was a lot more successful with his harmonica-driven treatment of Lee Hazelwood's This Town. He made Frank sound as contemporary as Riddle had done on Strangers. And why, when it was released as a single, it didn't make a higher chart position than forty one was a mystery to everyone at Reprise. The album was rounded off by the relatively old-fashioned, but superb Claus Ogerman treatment of Drinking Again which Frank had recorded on 1 February, and a very funny H B Barnum version of Some Enchanted Evening. Barnum's arrangement of Rodgers and Hammerstein's song seemed an incongruous way to follow the quiet sadness in Mercer and Tauber's saloon song, but the humour was important in modernising the tune. The finished product sure sounded odd, though. The album, simply titled Frank Sinatra, peaked at twenty four. when released in September.

FRANK AND THE DUKE
August–December 1967

FRANK HAD become Tony Rome. A tough, cynical private eye in the Sam Spade mould, but very much a man of his time, Rome was another perfect Sinatra front. Determinedly on the side of Right, he was willing to use any means possible to achieve justice as he saw it. Sid Korshak's friend Jill St John played the love interest to great effect, Frank got to joke, hit people and be romantic: some might say perfect typecasting. Whatever, Frank was once again filming, recording and then playing live dates in Miami, Philadelphia, Chicago and Vegas. He was getting bushed. During a two-week stint at The Sands he developed Vegas throat and had to lay off. A doctor said he was close to getting pneumonia, too. Still, he could play the tables. Except, he couldn't really. When Frank won, he'd take the money like everyone else. When he lost he figured the house he owned part of could stand it. But that wasn't the way house manager Carl Cohen saw it, so he stopped Frank's credit. Unfortunately Jack Entratter didn't want to tell Frank, so the first the Chairman knew of it was when he'd got these astronauts with him at a table – guys like Jack Swigert and Walt Cunningham who'd been out of this world, literally – and the croupier told him he hadn't got any credit. Frank snapped. He drove a golf cart through a window, ripped up the phone switchboard and confronted Cohen. Unfortunately for Frank, Cohen was 18 stone and BIG. Frank lost two teeth caps and a lot of face. But Frank was a big man too, so he got over it, telling Kirk Douglas he had learned to 'never fight a Jew in the desert'.

After this, Frank wanted to kick back with his wife, so he arranged for Mia to be in his new movie, The Detective, a tough film about bisexuality, murder and compromise. Mia though, was on set with Roman Polanski making some dumb horror movie called Rosemary's Baby, and refused to join Frank. What could a guy do? Just as with Ava and Juliet, he had to act the man, so he sent word that their marriage was over. Jacqueline Bisset took Mia's role.

The day before Frank's 52nd birthday, he was in the studio with a dream pairing – Billy May and Duke Ellington. Like he had with Basie, Frank had wanted to record with Ellington since he could remember. In truth both men knew the music they were making was long past its peak, just too old. Nobody wanted Swing any more, even if it was played by giants of the genre. The Jazz world had moved into the rock and soul area, the Beatles and the Beach Boys had just changed pop music forever with weird, exciting records (Sgt Peppers Lonely Hearts Club Band and Pet Sounds respectively), Americans were dying in Vietnam while listening to the Doors and James Brown. Who wanted a slow, downbeat version of Buddy Hebb's Sunny, even with the legendary Johnny Hodges playing on it? The answer was not many people. Which was a shame, because Frank was in a subdued but heart-felt mood, clearly aching over Mia on Herbert and Dubin's Indian Summer and feeling reflective on the Duke's own I Like The Sunrise. The eight songs recorded over two days are quiet, tasteful Swing ballads, beautifully arranged and played. But no-one was listening. The record Francis A & Edward K would make a pathetic seventy eight on the album chart when released in February of the next year.

CYCLES
1968

AS WAS BECOMING customary, Frank began the year in Miami at the Fountainbleau. He stayed through to April to film a second Tony Rome movie, The Lady In Cement, alongside Raquel Welch, a pretty young actress who'd been in several Elvis movies, most famously Roustabout. Man, she filled a swimsuit. Frank continued his residency after filming. In May he announced his support for vice-president Hubert Humphrey's play for office after LBJ refused nomination. He was up against Bobby Kennedy. In June, Bobby was shot dead. Frank continued campaigning for Humphrey.

In July Frank recorded Kaempfert, Rehbein and Sigman's My Way Of Life, and Gayle Caldwell's Cycles as a single, with Don Costa. Cycles, with its softly honky-tonking piano, restrained backing chorus and acoustic guitar sounded almost like a Country song – a genre

Frank had always resisted. Don Costa was on the ball, of course. The American rock world and Vegas were just getting into Country songs in a big way. The session wound up with a number planned for a new Christmas record, Jim Webb's Whatever Happened To Christmas.

In August he took Nancy Jr, Frank Jr and Tina into a studio with Nelson Riddle to record more tracks for the Christmas album.

Toward the end of August, some creep named Nicholas Gage wrote a piece in the Wall Street Journal linking Frank with every major Mob player there'd been. And again, the Democratic party advised their mainman, Humphrey, to stay away from the Sinatra name. Sid Korshak pointed out to Frank that they just used him and ditched him again. Maybe he'd be better off with guys who would take a stand on his behalf rather than running. To end the summer on a real downer, Mia flew to Mexico and got a divorce. Once again Frank was a man alone. It was time to make a new record – one with some sad songs on it.

As usual, at 8pm on 12 November, Studio One was packed with visitors and musicians. Among them sat a thin young man looking nervous, his hand being held by a beautiful young blonde. Beatle George Harrison and wife Patti sat staring as Frank worked his way through Bobby Russell's Little Green Apples, the melody accentuated by a tinkling piano and sweeping strings, John Hartford's Gentle On My Mind and Jimmy Webb's magnificent By The Time I Get To Phoenix. The sound was contemporary – West Coast laid-back hip, but unmistakably Sinatra. Harrison expressed his amazement at the speed with which Frank worked. Didn't the kid know a natural when he saw one? Some time that night, fat weirdo Tiny Tim also dropped by. What a freak. The next night Bill Miller ran the orchestra through Don Costa's arrangements of Little Green Apples again, this time successfully. They also finished Gary Bruce's Moody River and Gorgoni and Taylor's Pretty Colors, both with an unobtrusive chorus behind

Frank's laid-back delivery. The sessions concluded on the third night with Randazzo and Pike's Rain In My Heart, Gayle Caldwell's Wandering, and a sad version of Joni Mitchell's Both Sides Now. It was the one track besides Cycles in which Frank emoted.

After some scary stats from UCLA, Frank decided to move to Palm Springs permanently because of rising smog levels. Immediately though, Frank had to be in Vegas. Fuck The Sands, Frank was appearing at a huge hall of a room called Circus Maximus in Caesar's Palace, just down the Strip. They loved Frank so much that the management had medallions pressed with his head on it and an inscription which read, The Noblest Roman Of Them All. Man, they were raking it in when Frank appeared. The year was starting to look up, just as it was ending.

MY WAY
30 December 1968-March 1969

FRANK WAS AT Caesar's when he heard the French version of My Way, then titled Comme d'Habitude (As Usual), written by Claude François Ravaux and Gilles Thibault. Paul Anka, a former pop star himself, had 'interpreted' lyrics which Frank just knew could have been written for him personally. It was a classic French Chanson number full of big

themes like death and sorrow, in which a man sounded as if he had reached the final stage of acceptance about his own mortality. Yeah, Frank had a few regrets, yeah, he'd done what he had to do, he'd even taken the blows and, as his records showed, he did it his way. The opening lines held no fear for Frank. As usual he took the song head on, turning in a bravura performance for Don Costa. No other numbers were recorded on the day, 30 December.

In January Frank's father Marty was admitted to hospital with chest pains. For five days Frank watched him die.

Less than three weeks later Frank was in the studio with Antonio Carlos Jobim and an orchestra conducted by Morris Stoloff to record a follow-up to his and Jobim's previous, successful collaboration. Jobim's One Note Samba had an upbeat beginning, with Frank scatting along with the guitarist. The singer sounded slightly edgy, close to raw. On Jobim And Gilbert's Don't Ever Go Away the emotion really came through. Frank sounded like he'd been crying, and of course he had. He'd never talked to his father much, but then he didn't need to. They understood each other. Arranger Eumir Deodato used sparse, soft strings behind the voice and guitar. Jobim's Wave regained a little of the bossa nova of Girl From Ipanema, but had Frank reaching for low notes that were not easy. The day's session ended with an unsatisfactory Bonita, which was recorded the next day, along with three other Jobim tunes, Someone To Light Up My Life, Drinking Water and an unsuccessful Desafinado. On 13 February the troupe recorded Jobim's Triste and This Happy Madness, along with Song Of The Sabia. Frank knew the recordings

MY WAY FRANK SINATRA
ARRANGED AND CONDUCTED BY DON COSTA
MRS. ROBINSON
YESTERDAY
FOR ONCE IN MY LIFE
HALLELUJAH, I LOVE HER SO
WATCH WHAT HAPPENS
IF YOU GO AWAY
DIDN'T WE
ALL MY TOMORROWS
A DAY IN THE LIFE OF A FOOL
MY WAY
K 44015 STEREO

were not up to the standard of their first collaboration, and held them back from release.

My Way had come out as a single and seemed to be selling well, so an album was needed to go with it. On 18 February he booked Don Costa to record some new tunes. Frank felt nostalgic. He went back to the sound which he loved so much. Costa almost became Riddle and ran the orchestra through a decidedly old-fashioned version of Gimbel and LeGrand's Watch What Happens, all swinging horns and finger-clicking rhythm. On Jim Webb's Didn't We he looked to Gordon Jenkins, using solo piano and soft strings to set up the song of regret, joining Frank's voice with a soft sax and sad violin. Ray Charles's Hallelujah I Love Her So got the Billy May treatment, opening with a big fanfare before settling into a cod-R&B swing. Frank had liked Lennon and McCartney's Yesterday ever since he'd first heard it, and imagined it in the style of Axel Stordahl. Costa obliged. Sammy and Jimmy's All My Tomorrows was almost indistinct from the Nelson Riddle version of 1958.

The second side of the album contained the new songs, beginning with the epic My Way. The French Chanson feel was continued with Sigman and Bonfa's A Day In The Life Of A Fool, a sad song of a lonely man lost in love, with Frank positively feeling the line 'alone in my room I cry tears of goodbye'. Stevie Wonder's For Once In My Life, recorded in the same session as Watch, Hallelujah and Simon and Garfunkel's Mrs Robinson, was another Riddle pastiche. The most powerful number of the whole album was undoubtedly Rod McKuen and Jacques Brel's If You Go Away. Costa's accompaniment, with its low, tinkling harpsichord and soaring strings, perfectly coloured the background for Frank's full emotional phrasing. The song had to be recorded at the end of a night's work. Frank wasn't capable of continuing after that. As it had throughout his career, a song gave vent to his deepest held feelings. Frank had been left again, this time for good. Yet all the lingering feelings seemed to be good ones. As if scared of the effect on people of ending the album with the song, My Way closed with the upbeat Mrs Robinson, done in a Nelson Riddle-manner.

A MAN ALONE
March 1969

ROD MCKUEN WAS impressed that Frank Sinatra wanted to work with him. So he selected a dozen songs which Don Costa arranged and, over three days in late March, they were recorded. McKuen was a devoted fan of the French song tradition known as Chanson, chief exponents of which were Edith Piaf, Charles Aznavour and Jacques Brel (a Belgian). Chanson songs told stories, mostly about doomed lovers, killers and suicides in a typically French manner. Brel had made the form strictly personal, almost autobiographical and, at the same time, spiritually uplifting. McKuen sought to do the same. Just as with many other of his favourite songs, Frank felt the lyrics spoke for him. He knew love seldom worked out the way it seemed, as the title track said. McKuen was caught unaware by Night, as were most Sinatra fans, since Frank didn't sing on the song but simply spoke the two verses. He did the same on Promise To Promise, Out Beyond The Window and Some Travelling Music. I've Been To Town, with it's clichéd sax opening, felt like a good saloon song, speaking of a world that had broken down. All the numbers were world-weary with a lot of cynicism, but to Frank's mind they were ultimately hopeful. Frank didn't know what an Existentialist was, but McKuen did, and Frank was it.

A Man Alone was the darkest Frank had felt since No One Cares.

At the end of the week, Frank pulled out of Reprise completely, and made $22,500,000.

Which just showed what a little loneliness could do.

WATERTOWN
Summer 1969

IN MAY FRANK was back at Caesar's doing what he loved best. Except, he wasn't enjoying it as much. He had no father, no wife, not even a business anymore. Hell, he wasn't busted flat, but what was he doing? He was going to be 54 this year. In June Judy Garland died, broke. Frank paid for the funeral. Around that time, he met and became pals with an old pal of Sid Korshak's, Spiro Agnew, Richard Nixon's vice-president. In August Frank got together in New York with some new guys, arrangers Charles Calello and Joseph Scott for a new concept album, Watertown. Written by Bob Gaudio and Jake Holmes, the album was a kind of musical soap opera, with Frank as the central character. Except there was no plot. Frank sounded unconvinced on the songs, all of which seemed to be about the same thing, namely a guy losing his broad. The album was supposed to centre around a small town in New Jersey. Frank sounded as tired as the idea.

He should have stuck with Costa, with whom he'd made two great tracks a week earlier, Randazzo and Pike's Forgot To Remember and Randazzo and Weinstein's Goin' Out Of My Head. That would have been a better way to wrap up recording for the year. Instead, the last time Frank made it into the studios in the 1960s was to put the vocal over an orchestral track of Lady Day which Costa had already laid down in tribute to Billie Holiday. The decade closed with another legal argument over whether Frank should appear before yet another State Investigation Commission to discuss Mafia matters. Frank was more than a little tired.

SINATRA & COMPANY
1970

DUMB FILMS, LIVE shows in Vegas, recording dates and appearances before dumbass politicians intent on raising their profile at his expense – the year stretched ahead of Frank, just as so many had done previously. The old guys from back East were tired. Dino and Sammy were the same as ever, they still had fun, but at a slower pace now. The made men had moved away from the old pastimes. Drugs were everywhere, screwing up the kids. The war was still going on and the Democrats didn't have a snowball's chance in hell of ever being elected. Frank needed something new. The fucking State Investigation had him kept out of Nevada until he'd told them exactly the same stuff he'd told all the other wiseasses. Sure he'd met Meyer Lansky and Lucky Luciano, which performer in Vegas and Hollywood hadn't? As far as he knew, Jilly and Sam were not members of La Cosa Nostra or the Mafia. So the investigators let Frank go – after they'd asked if it was really him running for the train at the end of Von Ryan's Express. Assholes.

A week later Frank was in Tucson making Dirty Dingus Magee, a comedy Western with George Kennedy. Hell, it wasn't Cat Ballou, but it was fun, it kept his mind off things. Maybe he should go to Britain soon, that always made him feel better.

In May Frank and the Basie band played what Sinatra aficionados claimed were two of the concerts of his life at the Royal Festival Hall in London. Frank knew they were good, too. But no-one taped it.

Back in California, Frank came out in support of Ronald Reagan as State governor. He'd had enough of the Democrats for, as Sidney Korshak had remarked, what had they ever done for him? It stuck in his craw a bit to go for Reagan, but Frank, ever the pragmatist, swallowed it and sang for the old bird.

In September at Caesar's, casino manager Sanford Waterman pulled a gun on Frank in his office. Jilly Rizzo grabbed the old man's pistol after Frank told him where he'd stick it. The whole world was going screwy on him. Where was the respect?

In October, Frank finished Sinatra and Company with arranger Don Costa. John Denver's Leaving On A Jet Plane and his godson Paul Ryan's Drink The Wine were the debatable highpoints. Frank was tired, and he knew he sounded it. He couldn't stretch for the notes, or turn the phrases into gold. It was a real record of two halves, the first side being songs recorded with Jobim and Deodato back in February 69. At least the year ended on a high note, with Frank giving Nancy Jr away to her second husband, Hugh Lambert on 12 December. It was Frank's 55th birthday.

GOODBYE AND AMEN
1971

FRANK WAS 55, but he'd seen more life than a guy of 105. The time was right to get off the road. His family knew in March. The world knew as he picked up an Oscar for his humanitarian work, and set up a farewell concert to benefit the Motion Picture and Television Relief Fund at the LA Music Centre. It was a great night, almost good enough to persuade Frank that he was making a mistake. The songs were his personal favourite numbers: All Or Nothing At All, I've Got You Under My Skin, I'll Never Smile Again, Ol' Man River, That's Life, Try A Little Tenderness, Fly Me To The Moon, Nancy, My Way, The Lady Is A Tramp and Angel Eyes. Like so many live Sinatra performances before, the night was taped, and then never issued. It was a good time to go. Watertown had only made a lousy 101 in April last year, whereas Sinatra and Company had managed seventy four. The Mafia allegations were building again in Washington and the press. Dirty Dingus Magee was as bad as Frank had looked in the film. Ah, forget it. Goodbye and Amen to all that. Time for painting, reading, playing golf and helping a few people.

THE COMEBACK YEARS

OL' BLUE EYES IS BACK
April-August 1973

FOR THE FIRST year of retirement Frank kicked back. He slept some, hung out with the guys, drank with Dag and Sammy, played golf, moved Barbara Marx into his life and took a long, cold look at things. Ronald Reagan was moving ever higher in politics. The Democrats were looking more and more deadbeat, but didn't ask Frank to help. Meanwhile Vice-President Spiro Agnew, who Frank had met back in 1969, was coming on to him. Agnew was an old friend of Barbara and her husband Zeppo, who'd introduced him to Frank.

By 1972, the Republicans were approachable, and Nixon was the only electable option. Naturally Frank wanted to be with winners. Maybe he'd even get to be something like an Ambassador.

But first he had deal with yet another Congressional State committee – this time in New Jersey. Some ratfink in jail had said Frank was fronting a betting scam for the Mob. The guy was doing time for murder – several murders, in fact – yet the committee guys believed the bum, just

because he'd fingered Frank Sinatra, and everyone knew he was in bed with the Mob, right? Well fuck them.

Frank flew to England after he heard about the subpoena, and went to the races. When they dropped the order and started being nice to him, he flew back and went to see the Commission in Washington. They ended up apologising to him.

At the party after, Spiro told him Nixon sent congratulations. Did he want to meet the Prez? Frank came out for Nixon in the run-up to the 1972 election. Everyone said it was the right thing – Sidney Korshak, Barbara, Jilly. So his kids didn't agree, well, that was life. He'd already re-named the guest room at Palm Springs the Agnew room on account of the number of times Spiro ('Ted') and Judy had slept there.

Frank might have retired from singing, but the newspaper gossips kept haunting him. One broad kept sniping about Frank's new political friends. Then one night at a cocktail party in Washington the same broad started harassing Barbara for info on Frank. He saw it happening across the room, went over and slammed two dollars in the reporter's drink. 'You're a two dollar broad,' he told her, 'That's all you're worth, that's all you'll ever be worth. Go home and take a bath, you stink.' The next day Henry Kissinger called Frank and told him, 'You overpaid her'.

On 17 April 1973, with Barbara (now divorced from Zeppo) watching alongside

Nixon and Agnew, Frank came out of retirement at the White House. He sang ten songs, among them The House That I Live In, with Nelson Riddle leading the band. Nixon told Frank he should get out of retirement. Frank was always the sucker for a powerplay and on 30 April he went into Studio One in Hollywood with Don Costa to record Kris Kristofferson's Nobody Wins and Joe Raposo's Noah. It was not a good day, things didn't feel right, and sure as hell didn't sound right. Frank didn't want them released.

For a month Frank worked with Costa and Gordon Jenkins on a number of songs and arrangements, trying to decide what he was doing, how he would sound and who Frank Sinatra would be this time. On 4 June he and Gordon Jenkins filled Studio 7 at Hollywood's Goldwyn studio with an orchestra and band, then tried out with Sonny Bono's Bang Bang. It was pure candy-sugar, it just didn't work. Joe Raposo's You Will Be My Music did come together, though. The strings swelled, and grew just like they had fifteen years earlier when the two men had made No One Cares. As Frank's voice filled the air, the strings and thin reeds fluttered around his almost youthful baritone. Frank held the notes, stretching the words in the way only he could. An electric guitar barely impinged on an otherwise acoustic backing. The song set up the new Sinatra – or Ol' Blue Eyes, as he was to become after the marketing men had their way. This was not a man alone, or a man mortal enough to be hurt by another person, this was Sinatra the Singing God, the Legendary Entertainer. Ol' Blue Eyes wasn't old, he was as immortal as all the songs everyone knew and loved. This album was affirmative proof that Frank could cheat time. The songs might be sad, but they expressed a newfound certainty: Raposo's Winners was a call to arms for the disaffected to overcome negative thoughts; Caraveli, Jourdan, Anka and Sammy Cahn's Let Me Try Again an order, not a plea, to do it one more time, the right way; and Kristofferson's Nobody Wins a level acceptance of the end to a love affair, which said 'there'll be another'. Sondheim's Send In The Clowns was a piece of musical theatre – a tragic song which ultimately offered hope ('well maybe next year'). Raposo's There Used To Be A Ballpark was a song of joyful remembrance, full of evocative images and familiar sounds, in which Frank constructed a world that in truth never existed, but everyone liked to recall anyway. It was the definitive song of the new era and it was told by Frank, the wise storyteller. No drinks, no regrets. This time he was approachable, loveable. Ol' Blue Eyes. Like no All-American, all-knowing Uncle Disney that had ever existed.

As he was recording his comeback album, the Republican party were saying goodbye to their president and his deputy. For a brief moment during the Watergate investigation, Frank's name was mentioned along with others (including Reagan) as benefiting from tax concessions handed out by Nixon. It was bullshit and nothing more was made of it. But again Frank had lost out on the big scene. He stayed as loyal as ever to Agnew, campaigning alone to have him reinstated. America had been disgraced once more. Again, it seemed, the world needed Frank Sinatra to be there, to remind them of the great possibilities the American Dream held. They could all take note of his meteoric rise from truly humble beginnings to Untouchable superstar.

The new Frank, the wholesome one, was no longer the Chairman of The Board. He would kick all those bums out of Vegas. Presley had declared himself the King of Rock'n'Roll, wearing all that ridiculous gold flash trash around his expanding gut while strutting around Frank's room. What planet did Presley think he was on, playing that Thus Spake Zarathustra shit before coming on? All Frank needed to slay 'em was the great songs – the music which moved people, made them cry, laugh, love and lose. Frank was going out on the road again. He was back with more energy, more ideas and more great music than people had heard for years.

The dream team – Frank, Lady Ella and the Count. People paid up to four times face value for tickets to the shows.

SOME NICE THINGS I'VE MISSED
December 1973-September 1974

You Turned My World Around
Sweet Caroline
The Summer Knows
I'm Gonna Make It All the Way
Tie a Yellow Ribbon
Round the Old Oak Tree
Satisfy Me One More Time
If
You Are The Sunshine of My Life
What Are You Doing
the Rest of Your Life
Bad, Bad Leroy Brown

BY EARLY DECEMBER, Ol' Blue Eyes Is Back made number thirteen on the album charts. Not bad, considering how different it sounded alongside everything else out there. Where the hell did these people come from? A man named Alice Cooper? Led Zeppelin? Pink Floyd? Jethro Tull? Jesus, what a bunch. Still, at least there were some songwriters left. The Beatles might have split, but McCartney and Harrison were still writing good stuff. Lennon had gone a bit weird, though. Yeah, Frank was gonna record some of the new songs he'd missed. Two days before his 58th birthday, he went into the studio with Don Costa and recorded Jim Croce's Bad, Bad Leroy Brown (with a vocal chorus which pushed the almost old-fashioned Rock'n'Roll beat along) and Floyd Huddleston's I'm Gonna Make It All The Way. The song itself was a sort of cabaret blues number and no doubt inspired by Staggerlee. It told the story of a bad, gambling fighter. Costa's arrangement made it sound like the theme tune to a bad television series. Frank did his best, but there was only half the menace of his version of Mack The Knife.

Frank knew it. That's why at the end of the track he barked – just like he had with Dagmar back in 1951 – but this time with a smile on his face. Hey, anything for a hit, right? I'm Gonna Make It was an altogether happier affair. With its rolling, tumbling guitar chords and almost Country melody, the song resembled Glenn Campbell's Gentle On My Mind. Frank had a little trouble rhyming splendour with window, but that aside, the song sounded more like a hit than Bad, Bad Leroy Brown ever did (in

fact, Leroy only managed number eighty three on the singles chart).

That Christmas Frank had his whole family, including Nancy, to stay at Palm Springs with him. It was a good way to relax and prepare for Vegas. On 25 January the whole of Hollywood was at Caesar's Palace to watch Frank's real comeback. Sanford Waterman had recently been indicted for racketeering, and the new management were real nice to Frank, so it seemed like the thing to do. The next day he gave Tina away to Wes Farrell at their marriage at the Palace. What a party that was! Two nights later, Frank had a severe case of Vegas Throat, and didn't show. Nor the next night. He made the 31st, but pulled out of the first week in March altogether. He had to get out of the desert, it was killing his throat.

On 9 March Frank opened his tour in San Jose with Gordon Jenkins conducting the orchestra. The set was full of Frank's favourites – Come Fly With Me, I Get A Kick Out Of You – mixed with new numbers he was about to record. He included Leroy Brown which was better live than it had been in the studio. On 8 April Frank played New York's Carnegie Hall, with all the proceeds going to benefit the Variety Club. Bill Miller conducted the set. Once again a live Sinatra show was taped, and once again it was never released. Frank found something wrong somewhere in the performance. It just wasn't perfect.

On 7 May Frank and Gordon Jenkins began sessions to finish a new album. Kicking off with Johnny Mercer and Jimmy Van Heusen's Empty Tables, the slow session produced David Gates's If and Alan and Marilyn Bergman and Michel Legrand's The Summer Knows for the album. Empty Tables itself was never used. Frank's voice showed signs of stress as a result of the tour, and not having any rest after Vegas. Jenkins's arrangements were as tasteful as they ever had been. Frank's reading of If was perfectly performed, though lacking a little in feeling. The next day Don Costa took over the baton. Frank came out with the longest 'ssss' in his career for Neil Diamond's Sweet Caroline, before recording Kaempfert, Rehbein, Carnes and Ellington's You Turned My World Around. Frank tried too hard to make Caroline sound like Diamond's original. It was one of the few times he would bring nothing new to a song.

A modern ballad in the mould of a Carpenters' song, You Turned My World Around employed all the musical tricks in vogue, with regular orchestral crescendos, plucking harps and soft passages countering the string swells. Frank's vocals completed the effect. So far the ballads were shaping up as the hottest tracks. When the sessions resumed on 21 May with Costa, things didn't change much. Legrand and the Bergmans' What Are You Doing The Rest Of Your Life, a lush ballad in the best Sinatra saloon tradition, provided the vocal performance of the sessions. It would become a regular addition to the live canon. Frank was at home with the song's sentiment, and the piano-led, sparse arrangement. The same night Costa pumped up his horns for another crass attempt at making a contemporary pop hit. Tony Orlando and Dawn had scored a world-wide hit with Brown and Levine's Tie A Yellow Ribbon. Frank was never gonna repeat that with an embarrassing, childish lyric about a guy returning from prison to his gal. Despite making it up like a Billy May number, the song stank. Adding a huge, ballpark scream to the song on the line 'The whole damn bus is yelling', made it worse. The session ended with Floyd Huddleston's Satisfy Me One More Time, a vibes-driven fast shuffle. Frank's voice had gained some depth – a little gravel rubbed against the muted trumpet that shadowed the melody. It had been a long night. In the middle of the final number, If You Could Read My Mind, Frank stopped the tape. Too many goddamned words. And his throat hurt. The next day Frank became a grandfather, when Nancy Jr gave birth to a daughter. Two days later, a happy Frank finished the album with the only really good upbeat number, Stevie Wonder's You Are The Sunshine Of My Life. The Don Costa arrangement, restrained but insistent with horns running the beat like a classic Riddle number, would stay with Frank for future live performances.

Which was where the man was headed. On 6 June Frank was back at Caesar's. This time the throat held up and the people couldn't get enough. The show was opened by Ella backed by Basie and orchestra, who then went on to back Frank. What a ticket - they were changing hands for up to $100 apiece in anticipation of the tour hitting the Big Apple. At Caesar's, Barbara, Jilly and Frank's warm-up guy Pat Henry had the same table each night with a path kept clear to the bar. Jilly made sure of that, and since he was about to face trial after a slight tangle back in May, no-one argued with Jilly. Especially when Jilly's boys formed a phalanx around Ol' Blue Eyes to get him onto the stage, the tables or the bar. Frank never missed Ella's set. She returned the compliment and then they'd end the show duetting on The Lady Is A Tramp. It was all quite something.

After Vegas, Frank hit Japan. Man, those audiences were polite. Australia, his next stop, sure as Hell wasn't. The press were everywhere, demanding a conference. Frank lost his temper and let them know what he thought of them. Parasites, bums, hookers and pimps were named, as Bill Miller got shoved around. Some union or other demanded an apology from him. From Frank Sinatra! He asked for one back, and was told his plane wouldn't be serviced and that he couldn't leave the country. It took the Prime Minister's intervention to lift the boycott at the airport. In the end, Frank's final show was televised for free. 'Hey,' Frank told an audience, 'all this stuff about me over here is pleasin' Nixon. It keeps him off the front pages.'

Before flying back to the US, Frank took a well-earned rest in Biarritz.

Back in the States, Frank played Lake Tahoe with Frank Jr and Nancy Jr supplying back-up. Cute. All three flew to Caesar's to perform with Woody Herman and his band. It was a gasser, and Frank decided to tour with Herman, right after he finished a recording session with Gordon Jenkins. On 24 September, they ran through three sad songs, Adair and Dennis's Everything Happens To Me, Legrand, Sigman and Barclay's The Saddest Thing Of All and DeLange and Brooks's Just As Though You Were Here. Of the three, only the last made it to tape. A classic Jenkins/Sinatra number, but the problem for Frank was it could have been recorded twenty years previously. He didn't sound like he had in 1954. His voice was frailer, the phrasing was all there, but the bright, steady tone denied the emotion of the original. Frank had been living on the road for two months, living like he had twenty years earlier, but now his throat wasn't as strong. His heart and head were as hard and contrary as ever, but the drinking, lack of sleep and belting out songs had taken its toll. So what could he do, except go back out on the road? Some Nice Things I Missed had done badly, reaching a high of forty eight on the charts, but demand for tickets to see Ol' Blue Eyes in person was as high as it had been at the end of the 40s.

THE MAIN EVENT
October 1974

THERE WAS A time when Frank wanted to play the lead in On The Waterfront. Back then, though, Frank wasn't acting his roles, he was living them. So Frank never had to say the line, 'I could have been a contender'. There was never a 'could have been' in Frank's life. Thirty years earlier New York had been in love with Frank, but it was a childish, teenage love born on a wave of immature emotions. This time the love was real, grown-up and carried on a wave of respect. Twenty thousand people thronged the Madison Square Gardens on 12 October to witness the return from the near-dead of a growing American legend. Sure, Frank was a fighter. He'd fought any man he'd had to – he'd also fought Government commissions, newspapers, studios, and time itself. Sure, sometimes he'd lost, but he'd always come back fighting. Like the Americans who had won world wars, Frank had seen it all, done it all, and succeeded against the odds. He was his own man, one who would send an old friend a blank cheque in times of trouble, but who would cut that same friend off with a turn of his head if there had been a betrayal of trust. Frank was a man of immense talent, and great emotions. He was a born fighter. Which was why the Garden was the right place for Frank to let New York in on the secret of his immortality: the music, the presence, the belief. Among the three-night sell-out crowds were Robert Redford, Walter Kronkite, Carol Channing. Frank was introduced by the legendary Gardens MC, Howard Cosell. The second night the gig was broadcast around the world. Frank was a champ. So they cheated a little with the album of the event, so what? Frank didn't want to sell his fans short. The first two numbers, The Lady Is A Tramp and I Get A Kick Out Of You, are from the 13th, but Let Me Try Again and Autumn In New York are from the 12th. The brilliant, hard-swinging I've Got You Under My Skin on the album was the one from Buffalo, when Frank ad-libbed the old line, 'Where does it hurt, baby?' at some poor dame screaming at him. The Woody Herman band were in great shape, even managing to make Bad, Bad Leroy Brown (from 13 Oct) sound like a number from the Fifties. The version of Angel Eyes was also from the Buffalo concert, when Frank allowed himself the conceit of calling himself one of the last remaining living saloon singers – alongside Tony Bennett and Drunky Martin. Frank set the scene for the crowd as Bill Miller played quietly behind him. 'He doesn't want any answers, he just wants to talk, and he nearly makes it but not quite.' The Buffalo Memorial Auditorium was magically turned into a tiny bar at 3am.

At the end of the song, Frank took a drink and claimed that it was tea. He then turned to the crowd and told them that he started in New York by taking a four cents ferry ride across the Hudson. He told the good people that of all the names he'd had, the one he was proudest of was Grandpa. He then launched into You Are The Sunshine Of My Life. What a player! In June Frank had toasted the birth of his first grandchild with, 'I wish her a hundred times the fun I've had, and one hundred times as many guys as I've had broads.' But that was Caesars Palace, this was national TV. The House I Live In (actually taken from a gig in Boston on 2 October) was introduced with a tale of how his father, 'God rest his soul', told him how America was the land of dreams. 'Hey it ain't perfect, but if it were it'd be no fun trying to fix it.' It was corny but real, a reminder of the anti-racist work Frank had done back in the War. From there Frank pushed the orchestra into My Kind Of Town, telling them to step on it. The song was a kick in the head to all those bums who accused Frank of being a gangster, as Frank emphasised – 'My kind of people, every inch of it my kind of town'. The last number, the Grandstand, or as Frank put it, 'the national Anthem but you needn't rise', the Sinatra sign-off which sounded like he'd always sung it, was My Way (again the album version was from Boston). As Frank finished the line 'so I face the final curtain', the crowd shrieked 'No'. Frank ignored it, there was no thought of mortality in his mind, the song's sentiments applied only to the last hour and to all the regular Joes out there who wanted to be Sinatra. As he broadcast the last line 'the record shows, I took the blows', Frank made to depart on the same note as he arrived: kicking, fighting, defiant and strong.

Now that made two great live albums.

EMPTY TABLES
January 1975-February 1976

IN DECEMBER 74, Frank had visited Nixon at home. A week later he'd helped carry Jack Benny's coffin. The year began with a residency in Lake Tahoe, then Caesar's, then back to Tahoe. Frank was playing the gaming tables, singing up a storm and having fun with Barbara. The Main Event album had only made thirty seven in the charts, but live ticket sales were booming. In the studio on 5 March, Frank laid down Paul Anka's Anytime, John Durrill's The Only Couple On The Floor, plus Sklerov and Lloyd's I Believe I'm Gonna Love You using Don Costa arrangements and with Bill Miller conducting. Neither Anytime or I Believe made much impact on the singles charts. A week later Frank couldn't bear to allow any of the three numbers he recorded – Hurricane Smith's Oh Babe, What Would You Say, You Are The Sunshine Of My Life and That Old Black Magic – to be kept. The rest of the year was mainly spent touring. A couple more recording dates were thrown in, one in August for a Gordon Jenkins arrangement of Legrand, Sigman and Barclay's The Saddest Thing Of All, and another in October for John Denver and Joe Henry's A Baby Just Like You. Frank had played some massively over-subscribed gigs with the bland, countrified Denver in August at Harrah's in Tahoe.

On Frank's 60th birthday, his daughter Tina held a massive party at her home. Ronald Reagan was among the guests. Sam Giancana wasn't. He'd been found shot to Hell in his kitchen in June, his mouth full of bullets – the sign of a squealer.

In January 1976 Frank recorded three new songs live at Caesar's. Two of these featured only the piano accompaniment of Bill Miller – Empty Tables (which he'd unsuccessfully tried two years earlier), and Stephen Sondheim's Send In The Clowns (the third was Bruce Johnstone's I Sing The Songs). Unhappy with the results, Frank booked the studio for February to redo them. I Sing kicked things off, warming Frank's voice for Tables. With its familiar piano intro and blue tone, Empty Tables could well have been included on In The Wee Small Hours. A sad, slow drinking song, Frank put in one of his best vocal performances in years.

The introduction for Clowns started with a monologue about the song, a first for Frank in the studio, although it had worked live. With only a piano backing, his voice emoted and carried the melody with remarkable clarity and ease.
The recording deserved to be a hit.

It wasn't.

Dino introducing Frank and fourth wife Barbara Marx to Caesar's Palace. Far left is Cary Grant, behind Dino is Milton Berle.

I LOVE MY WIFE
March 1976-March 1977

AT THE END of February Frank met with CIA boss George Bush to 'discuss international matters'. In March, after another Tahoe residency, Frank and John Denver made a TV special, using the Harry James, Tommy Dorsey and Count Basie orchestras. Give 'em some of that old-time music. In April Frank played a 3,500 seat theatre in Westchester, New York. He also met up with East coast royalty in the shape of Jackie O and the pianist Peter Duchin. In May Frank sued a bum for trying to write his biography and a couple of weeks later bought Barbara an engagement ring. In June he recorded Danny and Ruby Hice's The Best I Ever Had and Neil Diamond's Stargazer, using Don Costa's arrangements. Diamond and JR Robertson's Dry Your Eyes didn't make it to tape this time, so Frank re-recorded it along with John Denver's Like A Sad Song in September.

By which time there was a fourth Mrs Frank Sinatra. Frank married Barbara on 11 July. In November the old romantic pledged his love the best way he knew how, when he recorded Cy Coleman and Michael Stewart's I Love My Wife (with a Nelson Riddle arrangement). Despite not being written for him, it was a Sinatra song through and through. It wasn't unduly sentimental and in it the narrator admitted his thoughts might stray, but hey, the bottom line was that he loved his wife. Frank would sing it live at almost every gig he played from then on, treating it as if it were an integral part of some musical play he was starring in (the song was written for a musical of the same name, so why not?). Frank and his fans dug the irony.

Six months later, the one constant woman in Frank's life died. The plane carrying Dolly, his mother, crashed into a mountain. For the first two days after the plane disappeared, there was no word of what had happened. When he found out, Frank cancelled the Caesar's show which Dolly was flying to see, and returned to Palm Springs to grieve. Dolly had been Frank's inspiration throughout his life. The woman was so goddamned argumentative – she would only ever do what she wanted, Frank had to fight her his whole life – but that's why he loved her, because she had made him what he was. She gave him life and the will to live it as only he – and she – knew how. For the first time in his life, Frank couldn't find the song to describe the way he felt. All he could do for Dolly was agree to make a TV film of Contract On Cherry Street, which was her favourite book. In it, Frank played a cop fighting the Mob which, when screened in November, got rave reviews. Before then he'd agreed to record some disco arrangements by Joe Beck – which stank.

The disco version of Full Moon And Empty Arms was dumped, but a 'modern' version of Night And Day was released. It bombed.

In March, Frank and Nelson Riddle started recording a concept album, the idea being to only cut songs with the names of broads in their title. Only a version of Nancy – which was sad, slow and painful – Mandel and Mercer's Emily and Sweet Lorraine were put on tape. The album was never finished. It was a dumb idea anyway – who was gonna buy a Sinatra album these days? Frank headed out on the road.

TRILOGY
July 1979-March 1981

A 3-RECORD SET ON 2 COMPACT DISCS
INATRA   TRILOG

ST PRESENT FUTURE

FOR MORE THAN two years Frank hadn't committed any songs to tape. He'd tried in July 1978, when he took three Don Costa arrangements of songs – Irwin and O'Kun's That's What God Looks Like To Me, Berlin's Remember and Carol Bayer Sager and Peter Allen's You And Me – and recorded them. But nothing was actually put on tape. It just wasn't happening. The live shows were where Frank was at. The interaction with the crowd was just the way it used to be. On stage Frank was 35 again. He was kicking, swinging, drinking again and the people loved it. Time stood still out there. Audiences didn't expect to hear the perfect reed from Frank, but they wanted to see, be near, maybe even touch. Frank was cheating time on stage, he still looked like he had when those people watching were young lovers, and it was thanks, in part, to the music. Great songs, great arrangements, some of which had served him well for twenty five years now. Why disappoint people with studio work that just showed he couldn't hit and hold the same notes any more? Or could he?

In July 1979 Billy May worked up some scores for Frank. They looked good. Producer and old pal Sonny Burke, believing time had not changed Frank all that much, suggested a concept album. A triple concept album for Chrissakes, with each record representing different times; the past, the present and the future. The past and present were easy, Frank loved many great songs from the old days, and some of his current stuff he liked. The future was more difficult. How about a composer making it up? Frank suggested Gordon Jenkins, he could make a big, orchestral piece, full of importance – a kind of modern-day Gershwin affair.

The album was to be recorded in sequence. After two days of recording with Billy May, Frank didn't want to keep anything. In his head he heard The Voice, the way he used to be. On tape, he heard the reality, an older, less sure voice making out to Harry James and Tommy Dorsey-style arrangements.

The only song laid down during those first two sessions was Mack Gordon and Harry Warrens' I Had The Craziest Dream, a bluesy, trumpet-led number which had the singer as young and lovelorn. Frank was barely believable.

The next day, 17 July, he recorded Gus Kahn and Isham Jones's It Had To Be You, which May structured like a Riddle song, with strings and muted horn shadowing Frank's voice. This was more like it, Frank didn't have to try too hard, he could phrase it as he liked, without pushing too much. After three days, Frank had tried all the old stuff, but the Gershwins' But Not For Me and They All Laughed, Berlin's Let's Face The Music And Dance, Hammerstein and Kern's The Song Is You, Lewis and Young's Street Of Dreams, Mercer and Arlen's My Shining Hour and Rose, Eliscu and Youmans's More Than You Know had not been mastered. A month later, after a break in Monaco, Frank flew to New York and started in on the new stuff, this time with Don Costa in charge. Carole Bayer Sager and Peter Allen's You And Me started things nicely, Frank had a deep reverb on his voice and the strings were set way back. Rested, Frank reached for and held some high notes and bent some stuff like he hadn't done for a while. Feeling good, Frank reached for an amazing new number which had been written for a new movie. New York New York was Martin Scorcese's first musical and was set in the 1930s. Fred Ebb and John Kander had done a great job, the song sounded as if it had been written in the 40s. Frank knew it was about time he immortalised his home town on record, so the orchestra struck up the theme from New York New York. It was a great song, but it needed a great performance, and this wasn't it. They moved on to Legrand and the Bergmans' Summer Me, Winter You, a soft ballad with sighing strings and a favourite Sinatra sentiment, where lovers forgot the world and lost themselves in each other. The day's session ended with an uplifting, medium-paced MacArthur Park, Jimmy Webb's song of reflection and optimism. Frank thought of Barbara as he sang of Nancy, Ava, Mia and all the rest, sounding like the sixty-three-year-old man he was.

The next day, 21 August, with Eileen Farrell behind him, and an acoustic guitar alongside their voices, Frank eased his way through Kris Kristofferson's Beautiful For The Good Times. Farrell, with her strong, high-tenor voice, was not a brilliant choice. Although pitch-perfect, her unemotional harmonies detracted from Frank's gutsy approach. The selection of Irwin and O'Kun's That's What God Looks Like To Me was crassly inspired. Frank got to play the wise father over a sugary backing. Try as he did, though, Frank couldn't make an epic out of the song. At least it was short. The day ended with a slow, acoustic-guitar led version of the Presley/Matson number Love Me Tender.

Frank had heard Elvis laughing his way through the song in Vegas, and thought it deserved a big treatment – which Costa provided. The strings swelled, the vocal chorus swayed and swooned, Frank tried his damnedest to turn it intol a hymn to love. It was close. On 22 August Frank kicked off the day's session with an attempt at Isn't She Lovely, Stevie Wonder's nursery-rhyme tribute to his daughter. It didn't work, but set things up for the swinging arrangement of Billy Joel's Just The Way You Are, for which Costa put a bank of horns behind the melody, punctuating the lines with four-note blasts and swelling strings. In its author's hands the song had been a too-sweet confection of a number. Frank's version kicked and celebrated the love. Staying in the groove, Neil Diamond's Song Sung Blue got the same treatment. Again, the songwriter's original version had been a little too bland. Frank gave the nonsensical lyrics an edge. The blues bass pushed the melody along as an electric piano played jazz riffs, while banks of horns coloured the sound. Frank managed to make the words sound like they meant something.

After three weeks' more rest, on 17 September Frank was back in LA, in the studio with Billy May to attempt to relive the past again. This time it all worked. All Of You pushed along at an almost alarming rate, with the singer leading the rush. My Shining Hour, which Frank had almost forgotten existed, slowed things down again. It was a pleasant enough song, if a little unremarkable. Frank got to hold some long notes. More Than You Know kept things soft and gentle. The next day, things continued as they'd ended the night before. But Not For Me featured a vocal chorus, and horns muted like they had been when the Gershwins' wrote the song. The tempo was picked up for Street Of Dreams, May adding a burlesque-style drum roll intro, the insistent horns helping Frank build to a grandstand finish. It wasn't

quite up there with Tony Bennett's version, but then he'd recorded it when he was much younger. The day wrapped up with a song Frank had loved when Ella sang it. Somehow, he'd never gotten around to it. They All Laughed was so precisely structured that even May's honking horns couldn't quite drag Frank away from Ella's phrasing. Still, it worked.

Frank was in a good mood to start the next day. It was time to finish up some stuff, and swing. May's orchestration for Let's Face The Music was lush and full, with an insistent beat. Frank kept pace, phrasing every word perfectly and with an air of slight menace. This was no gentleman asking for a spin on the floor.

New York New York was completed. This time Pete Jolly was on piano rather than Vincent Falcone Jr who'd played last time, but who was conducting here. It was another defining Sinatra moment, possibly the last he'd know. The song might have been new, but it was vintage Sinatra. It seemed that cities were now doing it for him where broads had in the past. Frank loved New York, and this was the first song that allowed him to say it. And how. Five days after the session, Frank played at a very different sands venue – the foot of the great pyramid, in front of Egyptian president Anwar Sadat and several thousand others. Two weeks later Frank led the Columbus Day parade through New York with State Governor Hugh Carey. He then played a charity benefit, before heading back out on the road. At the beginning of November, Frank and Dino campaigned for Ronald Reagan in his bid for the Presidency. Man, Frank needed the week at Caesar's after that.

During a stint in Atlantic City, Ruby – Irwin Rubinstein – owner of the Dunes restaurant, died. Another good man down. On 3 December, Frank finished the Present section of Trilogy with a touching version of George Harrison's Something. It was Nelson's arrangement, the one Frank had been touring with for a while. Frank made

(above) Frank and Harry James performing All Or Nothing At All, forty years on.
(right) Frank and Tony, the last saloon singers.

a number one of one of the greatest love songs written in modern times. The inclusion of the word Jack ('You stick around, Jack, it might show') made the song uniquely Sinatra. The words echoed the kind of loser-barman conversation of so many of his favourite saloon songs.

Nine days later, Frank turned 64, and celebrated forty years in the business with a party that gave him the mother of all hangovers. It had barely cleared when he and Gordon Jenkins began the Future sessions on 17 December. At least, it seemed that way. Two days of recording with a 155-piece orchestra was hard work. It was an achievement, sure. But was it worth it? The end result is a dull, pretentious and overblown attempt at creating another Sinatra myth – taking Frank into the next century to give a mythologised version of his life and times. The space allegories were already twenty years out of date. Jenkins was a great arranger, but he wasn't George Gershwin. Frank tried his best, but even he couldn't bring this hokum to life.

SHE SHOT ME DOWN
April-July 1981

ON ITS RELEASE in February 1980, Trilogy made number seventeen in the charts, and gained largely good reviews – at least for the past and present sides. Frank went on touring the world. In January 80 he played to the biggest crowd ever gathered for a single performer, when 175,000 people turned up in Rio. Ronald Reagan made President, and John Lennon was shot dead outside his New York apartment building. Frank took on more bodyguards when in Vegas. The town in the desert was changing rapidly. The old guys were gone and the new places wanted goddamned kids and food inside the Casino. At 65, Frank was still drinking men half his age under the table.

Dino was turning up for gigs less and less. All he wanted to do these days was sit, drink and talk to no-one. The lazy bum. Caesar's asked Frank to become a 'consultant', for which he had to ask the Nevada State Gaming Commission for a licence. The Commission brought up some ratfink weasel who'd written a book about how Frank and Sam Giancana had run together, and how Frank had fronted for the Mob. Frank had the FBI release documents which proved he had been watched and taped, but nothing had ever come up that directly linked him with the Mob. There were pictures of Frank with some made guys backstage after a gig, but he was signing an autograph for Carlo Gambino's granddaughter, for Chrissakes. Frank got his licence, almost twenty years after giving one back. In March 1981, Reagan was shot by some madman. Earlier that month Frank and Sammy Davis had played a benefit in Atlanta to help catch the sonofabitch who'd murdered twenty-seven kids. The world was becoming a scummy place.

In April Frank and Gordon Jenkins went into a Hollywood studio to record Bang Bang (this time it stayed on tape), a new version of Everything Happens To Me (which didn't stay on tape). They also recorded The Gal That Got Away, using the Riddle arrangement from May 1954, which Frank had been using in live perfomances. Here it was slowed down and, as when it was played live, segued into It Never Entered My Head. Frank managed a time-defying performance, his

Frank in Mexico City, 1986. The song is all.

voice sounding like it had almost twenty-five years earlier. The album took the rest of the year to finish. Robin and Rainger's Thanks For The Memory, Jenkins's own I Loved Her, Wilder and McGlohin's A Long Night and South To A Warmer Place were recorded in New York in July. Of the bunch, A Long Night stood out as a classic Sinatra/Jenkins number.

Melodramatic strings opened the song, leading into Frank's dramatic reading of what was essentially another saloon song – its 'loser' lyric underpinned by a walking bass and its vivid imagery set off by an almost film noire counter-melody. Don Costa added his version of Sondheim's Good Thing Going in August, before Jenkins finished things off in New York with Phillips and Costa's Monday Morning Quarterback and Jules Styne and Susan Burkenhead's Hey, Good Looking in September. The album only reached fifty two on the charts.

LA IS MY LADY
April 1984

IN THE FIVE recording sessions between August 1982 and March 83, only two Sinatra songs were put out. Howe, Nittoli and Schroek's Here's To The Band was the A-side of a single which featured Jules Styne and Susan Burkenhead's It's Sunday on the flip. Frank knew that Here's To The Band was an old man's indulgence, but as they go it was a worthy one. Throughout his career, Frank had commanded the respect of all the musicians he sang with, because he understood their work and what they had to go through to make it. The song, recorded in New York on 25 January 1983 with Joe Parnello conducting his own arrangement, simply said thank you to all the musicians Frank had ever recorded, sung live and drunk with. Six days earlier, while Frank was recording a Don Costa arrangement, conducted by Parnello, news had reached them that Don Costa had died. He was 57. Tony Mottola took charge for the LA recording session on 23 February 1983, which produced It's Sunday, a slow, acoustic-guitar backed number which was suitably Sunday-sounding. The laid-back imagery had Frank cooking the breakfast, reading the papers and fooling with his lover to Mottola's Spanish-style guitar accompaniment.

In May, Gordon Jenkins died, aged 73. In July, Frank, Dino and Sammy spent a night filming a brief appearance in Cannonball Run II. That week, Harry James died. Throughout the previous three years Frank had watched a number of friends die. At the same time he seemed to be thriving – singing, receiving awards and being feted by some organisation or another. Why this was, he didn't know.

(left) Frank and Judy's little girl Liza on the road in 1986. Frank paid all Judy's death bills.
(above) Frank and Shirley MacLaine, duetting in 1986. A few years later she would write that touring with Frank at this time was as hard as it had been twenty-five years earlier. Meaning that he drank, swore and acted up just like he'd always done.

One thing was for sure, he was still in good voice. Good enough to make another album, anyway. On 13 April, Frank went into a New York studio with Quincy Jones, who had become one of the world's biggest-name producers, having navigated Michael Jackson through his multi-million selling Thriller album. Q pulled an amazing band together, featuring among others, George Benson on guitar, Lionel Hampton on vibes, Marcus Miller on bass and the Brecker brothers on horns.

Ironically, the album's title track, LA Is My Lady, was recorded on the first day, in New York. Frank figured LA was the only major city he hadn't made musical love to. A pity he couldn't find a better song in which to do it. The Bergmans, Q, Peggy Lipton Jones and Frank himself came up with a mangy, embarrassing confection of squelching synths, clumsy lyrics and insincere sentiment. Frank hadn't lived in LA for years, and had no intention of doing so, yet he had the cheek to end the song with 'I think I'll unpack my bags and stay a little while'. It wasn't the first musical deceit Frank had attempted, but it was the crassest.

Of the other songs, Legrand and the Bergmans' How Do You Keep The Music Playing, and Cahn and De Paul's Teach Me Tonight worked best – and they were not arranged by Jones, the first being by Parnello, the second by Torrie Zito. Frank mixed up the songs, using some new ones, and some old. Q made sure they all swung a little like they had done in he and Frank's sessions with the Count's in the early 60s. Where the band sounded like a 50s swing orchestra, things were good. When Q tried to inject some modern elements, things got snarled up. Why the hell bassist Major Mule Holley was allowed to grunt away in the background to Mack The Knife was a complete mystery. Frank had been carried away by Q's enthusiasm. He loved how the song swung, and he even came up with his own verse, a variation on the one he'd used live a few times. Frank name-checked Satchmo, Bobby Darrin and Lady Ella, being modest about his own ability to do the number any justice. Frank neutered the song. Where once it had been genuinely menacing, with its hitman imagery of blood and teeth, the jollified verses with their emphasis on Frank's new words turned the song into a mere ego-boost to Sinatra. If Frank realised, he never let on. In October 1986, he even re-recorded his vocal to make more of his tribute to other singers and band members. The album would be judged on the title track and Frank's version of Mack The Knife. Which was a shame, because the LA recording on 17 May 1983 gave Stormy Weather a beautiful, bluesy treatment and, along with other tracks such as Sammy Cahn and Saul Chaplin's Until The Real Thing Comes Along made LA possibly the best of the post-comeback albums. The album only made fifty eight on the charts when released later that year.

The last Summit meeting, 1988. Dino retired ill, Sammy was dying, Frank kept drinking.

AND ONE MORE FOR THE ROAD
1993

THERE WAS ALWAYS the music, the songs. The faces out front grew greyer, but they were still there. Through the hard times, all the lies, the accusations and worse, Frank's people stood by him. People came to see him wherever he sang around the world. It was the people who mattered, those who knew and understood that, like them, he'd faced the world square on. Even if he hadn't always won, he'd always fought. And when he'd lost, Francis Albert had sung his heart out, bled tears for them, and still managed to come through. So some bitch had constructed some lying biography. It was, as usual, half the truth, the rest a figment of her limited dumb-journalist imagination. If she only knew.

In 1985 Nelson Riddle died of liver failure. Then Orson Welles died on the day Frank was attending Yul Brynner's funeral.

By the end of 1986, he'd drunk, smoked and fought more than many of the people he'd known who were no longer around, and all he had to suffer was the occasional memory loss. The problem was, with so many song lyrics running through his head, how could he remember them all? Then, in early 1987 Frank had been operated on at a Palm Springs clinic to remove an abscess on his intestine. Hey, who needed to eat when there was so much JD to drink out there? It was close, but it wasn't gonna keep him down. Frank fancied a Rat Pack tour. The first for God knows how long. He'd get Dino and Sammy together for one last, long blow-out. Dino hadn't been too good recently, but then he'd gotten lazy. A few gigs, drinking and hanging out with the guys would do him good. Dino made four gigs before quitting, saying Frank was crazy. Ah, shit they'd go on without him. Maybe they'd get someone else to come along. Apparently Judy's little girl, Liza, wanted to come sing with the old men. Five gigs later, they let Minnelli join them. For a year the threesome played various dates, but with each show, Sammy seemed to get duller, the light in his eyes dimming.

He died on May 16 1990. Now there was just Frank and Dino.

In December of the same year, Frank turned 75, and carried on as usual – singing, drinking, talking, shouting, fighting. The world wasn't changing anymore, it was always Vegas time. The roar of the crowds kept Frank protected against illness, safe from the ravages of time which had so decimated Dino and Sammy. While those people yelled for more, Frank would give it to them. So his voice wasn't as hard, precise or clear as it used to be – it still sounded undeniably like Frank Sinatra, which was all that mattered to the people. The songs didn't change, they were all there like they always had been. A bunch of old friends who said more about the man than a thousand hack biographies.

When at home in Palm Springs, Frank and Barbara spent a lot of time with the remaining Hollywood aristocracy – Greg Peck, Cary Grant. Jilly was a frequent visitor until May 1992, when the fool crashed and burned in the white Jag Frank had given him. That hurt. A lot.

Then, in 1993 Phil Ramone came calling with Eliot Weisman, Frank's manager, to talk over an idea of recording a bunch of duets with people Frank didn't know, and had hardly heard of. OK, so he knew Streisand, Tony B, Aznavour, Liza and Nat's little girl Natalie, but who the hell were Bono and Kenny G? They didn't even have proper names. As long as Frank didn't have to be in the studio with these guys, then fine. They wanted Frank to do the same old songs in the way he had since the 50s, which was easy. Somehow they'd splice the duets together later.

So, in July 1993, Frank recorded a bunch of stuff he'd done so many times before and in the way he always had done. The Lady Is A Tramp, I've Got A Crush On You, Come Fly With Me, Witchcraft, even One For My Baby. That Phil Ramone was a great producer, he had Frank sounding just like he had way back. And the orchestra could almost have been led by Nelson Riddle and Billy May. Man! What they could do in the studio these days. All Frank needed was the mic, a music stand and the musicians in front of him.

On release in October 1993, Duets was a hit, selling five million copies worldwide. A year later Duets II was released to less acclaim. Who the hell were these guys daring to share microphone space with Frank Sinatra? Lorrie Morgan, Luis Miguel, Jon Secada, Chrissie Hynde? At least Frank Jr got in on the act. He'd been leading Frank's band on tour for years now, and hadn't sung for a while. It was hard to tell the two Franks apart on My Kind Of Town. What the hell – Capitol had made him a hit again.

IN THE WEE SMALL HOURS

FRANK SAT UP in his hospital bed, and looked around the room. So many goddamned flowers he could hardly breathe. He wasn't tired, he wanted a drink and a cigarette, but the bitch nurse wouldn't let him, and Barbara had agreed. What a fucking bore. What was left?

Reagan was all confused about things. Nixon was dead. Dino had gone. The bum died with a smile on his face and a drink in his hand. Sid Korshak had died just the month before, of a heart attack. Only he and Lew Wasserman were left from the old days. Frank was determined to outlive him.

Frank couldn't stand up on stage and sing for an hour any more. It was embarrassing the way he'd fallen from the stool in 1994. He'd had to call it a day after a Palm Springs gig in February 1995. It was a damned shame because Tony Bennett was becoming a big star all over again, and more and more kids had been turning up at Frank's shows throughout the 90s.

Now here he was, two years later, and the world had stopped turning. He was back in LA because Barbara had wanted to leave Palm Springs. The air still stank but what the hell, he wasn't going to have much more of it. Now he faced the final curtain, but he sure as hell wasn't gonna let it fall without a good goddamned fight. He'd get the JD himself.

With his drink and a Marlboro, Frank sat in his study, flicking through a picture book. Dino and Sammy goofing off, cigarettes in hand, drinks at their side, black ties all screwed up. Man, what a time they'd had. Presidents had wanted to be in his Rat Pack, all the dames in the world wanted to be his baby, all the gamblers wanted to play his tables, the losers wanted his benediction. His mother had met the Pope, his children had seen the world, his grandchildren were set up for life.

And there were still the songs. Out there on CD, on tapes, playing around the world, the sound of Frank Sinatra making love, losing, fighting, winning. As he left the stage, Frank told his last live audience, 'May you live to be a hundred and the last voice you hear be mine.'

That was the way to go.

P.S.

In the end, just after midnight on May 15 1998, Frank's heart gave out.
All the times that it had been broken over the years must have had
some effect.

Whatever else is written or said about him, whatever is questioned about
his life and loves, one thing will never be in doubt: Frank Sinatra was the
best mothering singer the twentieth century ever heard.

And that's a Goddamned fact, baby.

Ring-a-ding-ding.

Bibliography/Acknowledgements

Sinatra: The Man And His Music, The Recording Artistry of Francis Albert Sinatra – 1939-1992 by Ed O'Brien and Scott P Sayers Jr (TSD Press 1992) was invaluable. The work by Ed O'Brien and Scott Sayers in uncovering the facts of Frank Sinatra's recording schedule throughout his career was long and thorough. They succeeded where many employees of the individual record companies involved had given up.

Recommended reading

Sinatra by Arnold Shaw (Coronet 1968)
Frank Sinatra by John Howlett (Plexus 1980)
Dino – Living High In The Dirty Business Of Dreams by Nick Tosches (Doubleday 1992)
Frank Sinatra An American Legend by Nancy Sinatra (General Publishing Group 1995)
Legend – Frank Sinatra And The American Dream edited by Ethlie Ann Vare (Boulevard Books 1995)
Sinatra His Life And Times by Fred Dellar (Omnibus Press 1995)

Sources

All song titles and writers taken from sleeves, labels and The Music Of Frank Sinatra, part of An American Legend Collector's Edition (GPG 1995)

The Capitol Years – all facts taken from album sleeves, labels and liner notes contained in The Capitol Years 20 record Set, and confirmed by Sinatra: The Man And His Music by Ed O'Brien and Scott P Sayers Jr
The Reprise Years – all facts taken from album sleeves, labels, The Reprise Collection 4-CD box set and confirmed by Sinatra: The Man And His Music by Ed O'Brien and Scott P Sayers Jr
The Comeback Years – all facts taken from album sleeves, labels and confirmed by Sinatra: The Man And His Music by Ed O'Brien and Scott P Sayers Jr

FBI information found in His Way: The Unauthorised Biography Of Frank Sinatra by Kitty Kelly (Bantam, 1986)

The Voice (Musician's Press) by E J Kahn Jr
Sinatra! The Song Is You (Scribner) by Will Friedwald plus insert notes for various CD releases

Articles

The Exner Files by Liz Smith, Vanity Fair Jan 1997
The Man Who Kept The Secrets by Nick Tosches, Vanity Fair April 1997
Sinatra On Ten-Inch – Peter Paul Oprisko II, DISCoveries July 1989

FILMOGRAPHY

1935 Major Bowes Amateur Theatre Of The Air (with The Three Flashes)
1941 Las Vegas Nights (with Tommy Dorsey)
1942 Ship Ahoy (with Tommy Dorsey)
1943 Reveille With Beverly
1943 Higher And Higher
1944 Step Lively
1945 Anchors Aweigh
1945 The House I Live In
1946 Till The Clouds Roll By
1947 It Happened In Brooklyn
1948 The Miracle Of The Bells
1948 The Kissing Bandit
1949 Take Me Out To The Ball Game
1949 On The Town
1951 Double Dynamite
1951 Meet Danny Wilson
1953 From Here To Eternity
1954 Suddenly
1955 Young At Heart
1955 Not As A Stranger

1955 The Tender Trap
1955 Guys And Dolls
1955 The Man With The Golden Arm
1956 Meet Me In Las Vegas (guest appearance)
1956 Johnny Concho
1956 High Society
1956 Around The World In 80 Days
1957 The Pride And The Passion
1957 The Joker Is Wild
1957 Pal Joey
1958 Kings Go Forth
1958 Some Came Running
1959 A Hole In The Head
1959 Never So Few
1960 Can Can
1960 Ocean's Eleven
1960 Pepe
1961 The Devil At 4 O'Clock
1962 Sergeants Three
1962 The Road To Hong Kong (guest appearance)

1962 The Manchurian Candidate
1963 Come Blow Your Horn
1963 The List Of Adrian Messenger (guest appearance)
1964 4 For Texas
1964 Robin And The 7 Hoods
1965 None But The Brave
1965 Von Ryan's Express
1965 Marriage On The Rocks
1966 Cast A Giant Shadow
1966 The Oscar (guest appearance)
1966 Assault On A Queen
1967 The Naked Runner
1967 Tony Rome
1968 The Detective
1968 Lady In Cement
1970 Dirty Dingus Magee
1974 That's Entertainment
1977 Contract On Cherry Street (TV movie)
1980 The First Deadly Sin
1983 Cannonball Run II

PHOTOGRAPHS